THE ANATOMY OF GRIEF

Publication Number 1083
AMERICAN SERIES
IN
BEHAVIORAL SCIENCE AND LAW

Edited by
RALPH SLOVENKO, B.E., LL.B., M.A., Ph.D.
Professor of Law and Psychiatry
Wayne State University
Law School
Detroit, Michigan

THE ANATOMY OF GRIEF
Biopsychosocial and
Therapeutic Perspectives

By

ROBIN ANDREW HAIG
M.B., B.S., F.R.A.N.Z.C.P., M.R.C.Psych.

Consultant Psychiatrist
Department of Palliative Care
Royal Prince Alfred Hospital
and
Central Sydney Health Services

Senior Lecturer in Psychiatry
University of Sydney, Australia

CHARLES C THOMAS • PUBLISHER
Springfield • Illinois • U.S.A.

Published and Distributed Throughout the World by

CHARLES C THOMAS • PUBLISHER
2600 South First Street
Springfield, Illinois 62794-9265

© *1990 by* CHARLES C THOMAS • PUBLISHER
ISBN 0-398-05704-4

Library of Congress Catalog Card Number: 90-11083

Printed in the United States of America
SC-R-3

Library of Congress Cataloging-in-Publication Data

Haig, Robin Andrew.
   The anatomy of grief : biopsychosocial and therapuetic
perspectives / Robin Andrew Haig.
      p.   cm. — (American series in behavioral science and law)
   "Publication number 1083" — Ser. t.p.
   Includes bibliographical references.
   Includes index.
   ISBN 0-398-05704-4
   1. Grief.   2. Grief — Social aspects.   3. Psychology, Pathological.
4. Psychotherapy.   I. Title.   II. Series.
   [DNLM: 1. Grief.   2. Psychotherapy.   BF 575.G7 H149a]
RC455.4.L67H35   1990
152.4 — dc20
DNLM/DLC
for Library of Congress   90-11083
                                                                      CIP

FOREWORD

"Loss, grief, and restitution are universal phenomena which are encountered by every member of the human race, have major health implications and are the grist to the mill of the counselor or psychotherapist," writes Dr. Robin A. Haig in the opening chapter of this book on the anatomy of grief. All life is infused with grief, and one must do "grief work," as the process of experiencing the painful affects associated with loss or separation is called.

The recent news item that Milton Berle, following the death of his wife, sold their longtime home in Beverly Hills must have struck a sad but familiar note for many bereaved people. "I didn't have to sell the house," he said, "but there are too many memories there, you know, after being married 36 years." To cope with his grief, Berle sought a change of scenery. Others try something else. What is helpful for one person may not be for another.

In this lucid and informative book, Dr. Haig provides an overview of grief from psychological, social, and biological perspectives. Grief as a universal emotional and biological response to loss is distinguished from mourning, which is usually regarded as a social process with prescribed rituals. He describes characteristic patterns of grief in infants and adults throughout the life cycle, and in differing loss situations. He discusses grief counselling and therapy in normal and pathological grief.

Dr. Haig explores the relationship and similarities between grief and humor—socially, behaviorally, and at the level of the central nervous system. Just before undertaking this work on the anatomy of grief, Dr. Haig wrote the book, "The Anatomy of Humor." As Dr. Haig points out, the experience and manifestations of grief and humor may be viewed as polar opposites but may nevertheless share some features in common and interact in the individual.

In a chapter on mourning practices and the expression of grief, Dr. Haig presents cross-cultural comparisons in the expression of grief. The experience and expression of grief by the individual are influenced by the mourning rituals of a specific culture. One of the things that affect the way people react to bereavement are the rituals concerning death and the religious beliefs about death. In burial services the seed of hope is sown in the moment when the despair may be at its greatest. Many of the rituals of mourning, however, have now been abandoned: we no longer wear black for any lengthy period, if at all, and many people have abandoned the belief systems underlying prayers. As a result, many people today are bewildered and find it difficult to come through the grieving process. Indeed, people are often very isolated in today's society, and they do not have the support of others.

In a case of wrongful death, legal systems use widely varying philosophies and formulas to compensate families. These differences reveal a great deal about the attitude that each society takes toward the family as an institution and toward life itself. Under the laws of many jurisdictions in the United States, the grief of the survivors is a measuring rod in the amount of damages awarded in a legal action. They permit recovery not only for the loss of financial support but also for the value of the family services the deceased victim would have provided for the rest of his or her life, and the value to the family of the "lost society, comfort, care, and protection" that the deceased would have provided.

In an oft-cited decision, the Arkansas Supreme Court made a detailed and extensive analysis of the factors bearing on an award for mental anguish and the evidence to be admitted on the factors. The factors include the nature of the relationship between the decedent and the survivor, the duration and intensity of sorrow and grief, and the nature of the death.[1] The Vermont Supreme Court said that these factors do not involve such technical and scientific issues that a jury is incapable of understanding and weighing the evidence without expert testimony. The court said, "They involve matters within the common knowledge and experience of the jury. We believe that the jury can evaluate all the circumstances of the case and make a just award without expert testimony."[2] In neither case did the Court mention the duty in the law of torts of a claimant to minimize damages, such as by seeking professional help.

Among the obstacles to the resolution of grief are the mourner's efforts to avoid the intensely painful mental distress and the expression of

---

[1]St. Louis Southwestern Ry. v. Pennington, 261 Ark. 650, 553 S.W.2d 436 (1977).

[2]Hartnett v. Union Mutual Fire Ins. Co., 569 A.2d 486 (Vt. 1989).

related emotions. In *Macbeth,* Shakespeare wrote, "The grief that does not speak knits up to the o'er-fraught heart and bids it break." The avoidance of grief or denial of grief is responsible for a great deal of the physical and mental illness which occurs from time to time among bereaved people. While there is a place for tranquilizers or sedatives in this context, it is sometimes used to avoid grief. The habitual use of medication is fraught with danger; they may block the necessary working through of grief. The duration of a grief reaction depends on the success of the grief work.

The exclamation *Good grief!* may seem to be oxymoronic but actually it is not as paradoxical as it sounds. It's a roundabout way of invoking Jesus Christ. It's a variation of *Good God!* The grief referred to is that felt by Christians at the crucifixion of Christ. Since at least the 14th century, the faithful have spoken of this grief as metaphysically good for the same reason that they speak of Good Friday as good—because the sadness of that day prefigures the Redemption. Dr. Haig describes positive outcomes of loss which may result from a satisfactory resolution of grief.

RALPH SLOVENKO

To family, friends and clients who have grieved.
To Maria and the grieving monk.

ACKNOWLEDGMENTS

I would like to express my appreciation to Charles Wahl, who many years ago enabled me to study under his aegis and stimulated an interest in this area. I would like to acknowledge the major contributions to theory and research by John Bowlby, Collin Murray Parkes, and Beverley Raphael. My apologies go to Beverley Raphael for the title, which I had already chosen prior to my becoming familiar with her own major work, "The Anatomy of Bereavement."

Both the Editor, Ralph Slovenko, and the publisher, Charles C Thomas, have been helpful, courteous, and efficient and are to be commended.

I am grateful to the Hemisphere Publishing Company, Washington, for permission to quote from Erna Furman's chapter on Children's Patterns in Mourning the Death of a Loved One in *Childhood and Death*, Eds: Wass, H. and Corr, C., 1984, pp. 185–203.

I would like to thank my wife, Maria, for typing the manuscript and tolerating my preoccupation with grief.

R. A. H.

INTRODUCTION

This, books can do-nor this alone: they give
New views to life, and teach us how to live;
They soothe the grieved, the stubborn they chastise;
Fools they admonish and confirm the wise.
Their aid they yield to all: they never shun
The man of sorrow, nor the wretch undone;
Unlike the hard, the selfish, and the proud,
They fly not sullen from the suppliant crowd;
Nor tell to various people various things,
But show to subjects, what they show to kings.

The Library, 1.41
George Crabbe 1754-1832

It is discomforting to reflect on the probability that the longer we live, the more likely we are to experience grief, either in ourselves or in others, in response to the losses which occur throughout the life cycle. Life involves the experience of a series of losses which are akin to "little deaths."

My first remembered contact with severe grief in another was when I was four years old and a boy from next door ran, weeping, into our lounge. His youngest sister, doted on by the rest of the family, had just died from leukemia, after years of concerned care. Presumably, his parents were so absorbed in their own grief that he had to find solace in a neighbour's house. I did not understand what was going on, but watched with interest as my mother tried to console this weeping boy, who was normally a "tough guy." Gradually, the tears subsided, and after a time he was returned to his home, quiet and sad. I was told that little Brenda had "gone to heaven" and I subsequently reflected that heaven must be a ghastly place if it produced such distress in Brenda's brother.

However, a year later, when my Aunt Annie was dying, she could hear the angel choirs singing nineteenth century hymns welcoming her to heaven, so perhaps it was not such a bad place after all, although it probably had a musty smell like a church. My relatives who attended her death bed appeared to find the singing a source of comfort, although they were obviously having difficulty in hearing the heavenly hosts.

Death becomes more meaningful and grief a personal reality when relatives and friends die. It is difficult to envisage grief in its entirety until it has been personally experienced.

Subsequently, my interest in grief developed professionally in my contact with patients who have experienced major losses, through the burgeoning literature on grief and bereavement, both in children and adults, which has been extended by many eminent researchers, and through my own recent study of humor, its origins, and its use in therapy. The relationship between grief and humor becomes apparent in the use of humor to defend against the pain of loss and in the physiological and neurological processes that are common to both.

Grief may have important biological and social functions, although at times it may appear distressing and counterproductive. However, it may also be part of a healing force, which moves towards restitution and permits homeostasis in the individual and society.

Examining grief from biological, social, and cultural perspectives sheds more light on our understanding of grief and its ability to inhibit or promote health. Many myths about grief and bereavement are modified in this process. Psychoanalytic theory has utilised loss and grief paradigms as a basis for understanding many of the psychological conflicts of individuals and this has been employed in treatment. Ethological, cognitive, immunological, and chronobiological theories have all added to our understanding of the grieving process.

The epidemiology and pathology of bereavement have been widely explored and reviewed in recent years. I attempt to extract and summarise the core of these studies, which illustrate the range of patterns of grieving and effects on physical and mental health.

Understanding more about the grieving process has practical value for therapists, counsellors, and the health professional who encounter patients who are negotiating major losses in their lives. Counselling the bereaved and the management of pathological grief are valuable skills.

A range of treatments has been described in the management of pathological grief and severe grief reactions, ranging from psychodynamic to behavioural, pharmacological to cathartic, and scientific to inspirational. They may all be useful in selected individual clients, but should not be applied uncritically.

Grief is not necessarily a negative situation, although generating discomfort at the time. The outcome for the bereaved may be one of increased creativity, psychological insight, or toleration for the losses of others. An individual may emerge politically as a powerful leader, thus avenging the loss of a murdered relative (witness the rise of Sirimavo Bandaranaike, Corazon Aquino, and Benazir Bhutto, who all became national leaders).

Works on bereavement tend to fall into two categories, including those that sanitise the process and describe it in a detached way, and those that sentimentalise without objectivity and provide saccharine reflections. I attempt to steer a course between the two. In addition to examining grief in response to bereavement, it is important to consider the responses to losses of a lesser kind, which often involve a process akin to grieving in order to regain psychological and emotional equilibrium. Such losses include the loss of home, status, role, health, ideals, friends, or material assets. The discovery by a mother, that her favourite son is not heterosexually inclined but has "come out of the closet" and declared himself to be homosexual, may trigger a grief reaction. Orthodox Jews, who married outside the faith used to be treated by their families as if they were dead, were ostracised and relatives would be forced to grieve this loss. The "empty nest syndrome," when the children have left home finally, is but a variant of a grief reaction.

Having written "The Anatomy of Humor," it seemed consistent to suggest "The Anatomy of Grief" as a title. The two works complement each other in more ways than merely the title. An understanding of the therapeutic uses of humor becomes important in mitigating some of the pain of grief, and aiding the transformation of unverbalised affect into symbols which are meaningfully communicated to those around, thus helping to break and reestablish the bonds of human existence.

All good things must come to an end. I realised this at the time when I was writing the chapter on "Mourning," I was woken by a vivid dream in which I was being dressed in my best clothes by an attentive undertaker, who did not seem to be put off by the fact that I was not yet dead. He retorted:

> We do this all the time these days, Sir. People like to organise their wardrobes before their death. It's known in the trade as an anticipatory fitting. Yes sir, that stripy red shirt looks just the thing, but I'm afraid that your lounge suit is, well, too small and a little moth-eaten. You need an oversize jacket, as we like to put extra stuffing inside the shirt

and in the shoulders. It doesn't matter too much about the trousers, as nobody looks at that part of your anatomy.

In my dream I suddenly felt affronted, intruded on, and far too young to "bite the dust," and certainly had no intention of being stuffed by an undertaker. On waking, I realised that perhaps this was a timely reminder to finish the manuscript and return it to the publisher.

CONTENTS

THE ANATOMY OF GRIEF

Chapter 1

APPROACHES TO GRIEVING

Beside, as Plutarch holds, 'tis not in our power not to
lament: 'Tis a natural passion to lament and grieve. . . .

Robert Burton
1621

Loss, grief, and restitution are universal phenomena which are
encountered by every member of the human race, have major health
implications and are the grist to the mill of the counselor or psychotherapist. Life events involving loss (exit events) or threatened loss
are subjectively distressing and may precipitate depressive disorders,
attempted suicide, and anxiety disorders. Permanent loss is more likely
to be associated with a depressive picture, while a threatened or temporary loss is associated more commonly with features of anxiety (Bowlby,
1980).

Grief may be defined as the experience and expression of an emotion
which is deep and sorrowful and includes affective, cognitive, and
behavioral components, which follow a severe loss such as a bereavement.
This definition focuses on a personal experience which is inextricably
linked to its expression by the individual who has been bereaved.

Mourning is generally regarded as the socially sanctioned expression
of grief following a bereavement, which often occurs in a prescribed and
institutionalised way, with formalised rituals (see Chapter 7). Mourning
ceremonies may be participated in by some individuals such as distant
relatives who may not be experiencing the full range of subjective grief
reactions. However, psychoanalysts have tended to use the term mourning to describe the internal processes of grieving.

Bereavement describes the objective situation of an individual who
has sustained the loss through death of a close relationship.

Parkes (1972) has drawn attention to the reactions subsequent to
amputation, loss of a home, or migration which have some similarities to
a bereavement reaction following the loss of a partner. The characteristic

3

symptoms of grief and the maladaptive consequences will be described in subsequent chapters.

The results of working through a grief reaction and achieving restitution may be to strengthen adaptive functioning, to call on inner resources which were previously untapped and to utilise the social network and institutions of society in an imaginative and life-enhancing way. Creative identifications with the lost object (Krupp, 1965), an increase in creativity, joy at being alive (Paul, 1986), or a mellowing of personality and an increase in humanitarian values may all succeed bereavement. However, the detrimental consequences of bereavement, including long-term distress, suicide (Stengel, 1969), and an increase in morbidity and mortality all require consideration.

Death is no longer a taboo topic and this has led to an explosion in the number of published studies on dying and grief.

Psychoanalysts have examined the internal psychological processes of mourning and attempted initially to explain the phenomena of grieving in a closed framework with little consideration of the social or biological processes which were occurring. In the following chapters, that balance is redressed.

Social studies of bereavement focussed initially on spousal bereavement. A large number of widows throughout the world who experience some distress become a natural target for such research. More recently the area of the grief reactions of parents following the loss of children has been opened up. Other groups, such as homosexual men who experience various bereavement reactions following the death of friends from AIDS (Martin, 1988) and soldiers who lose comrades in battle (Garb et al., 1987) have come under scrutiny.

Bereavement researchers may encounter public prejudice or denial of situations which needs to be addressed prior to exploring potentially contentious or painful areas. Only a little pain can be uncovered at a time. Comparisons between groups who experience different loss situations such as widows and divorcees have been made by Kitson et al. (1987) and reveal differential reactions, such as greater grief in widows, and a greater likelihood for widows to seek professional help as a result of feelings of distress, whereas divorcees are motivated by anger to seek help.

Exciting developments have taken place in examining grieving from the ethological perspective and attempting to understand how *Homo sapiens* converges with lesser species in his reactions to loss, and the survival value which accrues for the individual and for the species as a result. Endocrinological and immunological research has also expanded our knowledge of bereavement and possible implications for physical health in a fascinating way.

Simpson (1987) rated the quality of books on bereavement and death, and considered that only a few were of outstanding quality, while many were mediocre and contributed little to a scientific understanding of the area.

Grief is unavoidable. Descriptions of it abound through history and in different cultural settings. At times it has been regarded as an affliction or a divine punishment, advice has been meted out by physicians and priests on its management, it has been studiously avoided, or has become the object of intensive scientific investigation.

Burton (1960) quoted Seneca who claimed that it was sometimes good to be miserable in misery and that for the most part grief evacuated itself by tears, but also referred to the advice of Germanicus, that we should not grieve excessively or to let the passions tyrannise.

Burton (1960) noted cultural differences in 1621 and commented that the Italians slept away care and grief, the Danes, Dutchmen, Polish, and Bohemians drink it down, while the English went to see a play. He also gave several examples of pathological grief reactions, including those of Niobe, who was stupefied by extreme grief, Aegeus who drowned himself after his son's death and a patient of Phalopius who was cured after growing desperate on his mother's death, but relapsed irrecoverably following the sudden death of his daughter.

Pigman (1985) traced the attitudes towards mourning during the last decade of the sixteenth and first decade of the seventeenth century in English literature. Open expression of grief was regarded as subversive of the rule of reason and social order. The bereaved were likely to feel that their grief revealed irrationality, weakness, inadequate self-control and impiety. The purpose of consolation was to suppress grief and to prevent the breakdown of the ideal of rational self-sufficiency. Some theologians at that time condemmed all mourning as evidence of lack of faith while others allowed moderation in mourning which hardly differed from a complete suppression of grief.

The attitudes to grief and its expression are diverse in modern societies. Even though an attitude to death and an after life may modify a grief reaction considerably, it seems that part of the grieving process is automatic and only partially under voluntary control. The associated affects, cognitions, and behaviors of grief (and endocrinological and immunological changes) always tend to occur to some degree, although they may be modified by social support, environmental cues, and previous experiences of grief.

Grieving is not a static phenomenon but a dynamic process. There is a dynamic interaction between the social, psychological, neuroendocrine, neurophysiological, environmental, and other systems. It is important not to oversimplify this process, but in order to understand and apply knowledge in a useful and therapeutic way it is necessary to focus on basic findings and extract some comprehensible principles.

In the following chapters, the areas of symptomatology, related morbidity, theory, biological aspects, pathological laughing and crying, the relationship between grief and humor, cultural differences, symbolic representations, personal development and attitudes to death through the life span, with attention paid to the role of play in this process, are covered. Sections dealing with the traumatic losses, including the loss of a parent in childhood and its repercussions, the loss of a child and maladaptive grief reactions lead into consideration of the management of the normal range of grief reactions, and counseling and therapy in those who are at risk or suffering from an abnormal grief reaction. The final chapter attempts to come to a resolution of the personal attitudes to death and grieving which have been expressed over the centuries.

Chapter 2

GRIEF SYMPTOMS AND ILL HEALTH

So grievous a torment for the time, that it takes away
their appetite, desire of life, extinguisheth all delights,
it causeth deep sighs and groans, tears, exclamations,
howling, roaring, many bitter pangs, and by frequent
meditation extends so far sometimes, they think they
see their dead friends continually in their eyes ... brave
discreet men otherwise, often times forget themselves,
and weep like children many moneths together.

The Anatomy of Melancholie
Robert Burton
1621

THE SYMPTOMATOLOGY OF GRIEF

It is a common observation that loss of a close relationship is often
accompanied by emotional suffering, an alteration in social functioning
and sometimes a deterioration in health. To describe these accompaniments as symptoms is suggestive of a disease process, as discussed by
Engel (1961). However, many of these symptoms diminish considerably
or cease after a time and may be part of the reparative or homeostatic
mechanisms which could be viewed as a naturally occurring part of
the human life cycle. Nevertheless, these reactions may be severe,
distressing, and impair functioning, and include alterations in appetitive
behaviors, circadian rhythms, endocrinological parameters, immunological
functioning, and mood and cognition. In most individuals the psychological components of grief are the most prominent and resemble those
found in depressive disorders. There may be an increased morbidity and
mortality at certain times following bereavement.

The immediate and short-term reactions to bereavement have been
documented and reviewed by many authors, although largely in Westernised cultures. Parkes (1980), Raphael (1983), and Osterweis et al. (1984)
all review the area well.

Lindemann (1944), who studied the aftermath of the Cocoanut Grove

7

Nightclub fire, described the grief syndrome as consisting of sensations of somatic distress occurring in waves lasting from twenty minutes to one hour, a feeling of tightness in the throat, choking, with shortness of breath, a need to sigh, an empty feeling in the abdomen, lack of muscular power, and an intense subjective distress described as tension or mental pain.

Glick et al. (1974) considered that the core reactions of grief were universal.

Maddison et al. (1968) in a postal survey compared one hundred and thirty-two American and two hundred and twenty-one Australian widows with a control group. Nervousness, depression, fears of nervous breakdown, feelings of panic, persistent fears, nightmares, insomnia, loss of appetite, loss of weight, and fatigue were all commoner in the newly bereaved group of widowers. These findings were reflected in a prospective study of Harvard widows by Parkes et al. (1980).

Clayton et al. (1971), in a prospective study of randomly selected bereaved persons, found that depressed mood, crying, and sleep disturbance occurred in the majority of subjects, while loss of appetite, weight loss, and fatigue occurred in half the subjects. Other symptoms which are often associated with depressive disorders occurred more commonly in the bereaved versus the nonbereaved controls during the first year (Clayton, 1974), although suicidal thoughts and psychotic symptoms were uncommon in both groups, except for auditory and visual hallucinations, which were experienced by 12 percent of the bereaved subjects but only 2 percent of the controls. These latter findings correspond with those of Rees (1971) in Wales in which two hundred and ninety-three widows and widowers were interviewed, some of whom reported hallucinatory phenomena of the deceased. Fourteen percent experienced visual hallucinations, 13.3 percent experienced auditory hallucinations, 11.6 percent conversed with the deceased, while 2.7 percent experienced haptic hallucinations (hallucinations of touch). Dreams about the deceased may be prominent.

Restlessness, yearning, and searching behaviors have been described by Parkes (1980). Anger is a common reaction to the death of a loved one and feelings that the deceased has "deserted" may alternate with feelings of panic.

An intense numbing often occurs initially following bereavement, when it may be difficult to accept that the death has occurred. This may only lift after hours or days when confronted with the reality of the corpse, postmortem, or funeral. Intrusive waves of distress then occur, with yearning, some emotional pain, active recollection of multiple facets of the deceased, and these waves may alternate with further episodes of numbness or denial. A powerful fantasy may then develop that the deceased is still alive and all is well, only to be replaced by the realisation of the loss subsequently.

In the early stages of grief, the individual may adopt a characteristic posture, with head slumped forwards in the hands, turning away from people and with subjectively experienced muscular weakness and sometimes the adoption of a "foetal posture." Contraction of the muscles around the eyes, a lowering of gaze, the raising of the inner aspects of the eyebrows, wrinkling of the forehead and the base of the nose and depression of the angles of the mouth accompany the characteristic vocalisations of sobbing or weeping and the production of tears. The vocalisations consist of a prolonged expiration (and low moan) with short, sharp inspirations. These vocalisations are the opposite to those found in laughter, in which there is a prolonged inspiration followed by short, sharp, staccato expirations.

Darwin (1872) considered that weeping was the primary expression of suffering in children, that sobbing was the partial expression of weeping, and that the contraction of muscles around the eyes was necessary to protect the eyes from the rise in venous pressure that accompanies forced expiration. He considered that the facial expression in grief resulted from a suppression of the impulse to cry aloud.

The expression of grief by weeping may sometimes be followed by a temporary feeling of relief. The expression of grief may help to confirm the extent of the loss, engage social support, and delineate the goals which the individual will ultimately work towards. Speculative suggestions that the tears contain or stimulate the production of endorpins which have analgesic properties have not been substantiated.

The symptoms of grief vary considerably in different individuals. The time scale for grief symptoms is also variable and is not completed within a few weeks, as early investigators thought, but often continues for months or even years, consisting of waves which may be triggered off by reminders or anniversaries. The more severe symptoms of grieving usually diminish over the first few months.

Zisook et al. (1986) developed a multidimensional questionnaire examining painful affects, coping strategies, functioning, continuing relationship with the deceased spouse, social relationships and changes in roles, identities, self-concepts and the world view. In a study of three hundred widow(er)s the course of grief was variable. The most affective distress occurred during the first month. However, after four years, several were still tearful and depressed. There was no change in identity or self-concept over time. After four years, the overall adjustment in 20 percent was poor and in 44 percent was excellent. Forty percent were living with someone of the opposite sex after four years. For many individuals, in spite of partial denial, which may be a coping mechanism, the memory of the deceased stays with them indefinitely.

The concept of fixed stages of grief has fallen out of favor with researchers. There is considerable overlap between the stages which have been described, although an approximate division into stages of shock, protest, despair, and reorganisation may have heuristic value.

Grief is a process rather than a steady state, one phase merging into another. Greenblatt (1978) delineated four approximate stages of grief, including one of shock, numbness, denial or disbelief, one of pining, yearning and depression, one of emancipation from the loved one and readjustment to the new environment and a final one of identity reconstruction.

The processes of grief may be cyclical in nature rather than sequential, with some repetition of pining alternating with denial, while readjustment to the new environment is being made.

The general trend of studies appears to have become more sophisticated, utilising standardised questionnaires, less diverse groups, prospective approaches, and matched control groups. However, many of the studies appear to have been conducted in Westernised societies. The standardised questionnaire or structured interview may sometimes miss out on detailed psychosocial data and does not always capture the subjective aspects which would be incorporated in a less structured approach.

Raphael (1983) pointed out that the two losses that the adult may experience which stand out as the most disruptive and potentially stressful were the death of a spouse and the death of a child. She described the complex dynamic of the marital dyad, which is influenced by past experiences with parents and others and the currently held fantasies of both partners. The reaction to the death of a partner is influenced by the current relationship and interlocking dynamics.

The reactions to the death of a baby are discussed in Chapter 11. The loss of a parent in childhood is discussed in Chapters 9 and 10.

PHYSICAL HEALTH AND BEREAVEMENT

Sleep disturbance and weight loss are commonly encountered after bereavement. Clayton (1980) found that sleep disturbance and weight loss occurred much more frequently in widows than widowers. Seventy-eight percent of the bereaved experienced sleep difficulties in the first month and 49 percent at thirteen months, while 40 percent experienced weight loss at one month and 52 percent gave a history of weight loss at thirteen months.

It has been suggested that there is an increased mortality and physical morbidity post bereavement. Maddison et al. (1968) found that 21.2 percent of Boston widows and 32.1 percent of Sydney widows reported a marked deterioration in health, with Boston widows tending to use alcohol more, whereas the Sydney widows were more likely to use sedatives. Using the self-report questionnaire in this study, it was not always possible to distinguish between painful affect, somatic change, or the assumption of the sick role. However, there was little change in the frequency or severity of major diseases postbereavement.

Clayton (1974) demonstrated no difference in the one year mortality in a group of older widows (the average age being sixty-one years) studied prospectively, with no difference in the number of physician visits, hospitalisations, or the use of tranquillisers.

Jacobs et al. (1977), in a review of the literature on the mortality of bereavement, found that younger persons and men were at higher risk, with the major effect in the first two years, but commented that the methodology of studies was varied and socioeconomic status and social stress were not well controlled as independent variables.

Helsing et al. (1981) in a prospective study of 4032 white bereaved persons demonstrated that there was no difference in the mortality of female widows and married controls but that there was an increase in the mortality of males over the age of fifty-five years. There was also a possibly higher mortality in the second year for widows under the age of sixty-five years.

Windholz et al. (1985) in their review of the literature found that both widows and widowers were at greater risk for the development of physical illness, while men who lost a spouse had higher mortality rates than controls. Morbidity studies indicated that both men and women who lose a spouse consult physicians more frequently, consume more psychotropic drugs (sedatives, hypnotics, and minor tranquillisers) and report poorer physical health on a variety of questionnaires.

Mor et al. (1986) found that in 1447 subjects who had recently been bereaved there was an increase in visits to physicians, but a lower than expected hospitalisation rate when adjusted for age and sex. Previous health problems and having been married to the deceased were the strongest predictors of morbidity and health care use.

Jones (1987) in a ten-year longitudinal follow up of 7,060 widowers and 14,900 married widows found that the widowers but not the widows had a 10 percent excess mortality rate. Some increases in death rates shortly after spousal bereavement were observed, with a twofold increase in mortality from all causes in the first month after widowhood. No peak of postbereavement mortality from malignant disease was clearly established in either sex.

The findings which were based on health questionaires do not always distinguish between somatic symptoms and psychological symptoms. Patterns of physician utilisation and medication use may represent psychological distress rather than a deterioration in physical health. However, there does seem to be an increase in morbidity and mortality, more pronounced in the early postbereavement months and particularly amongst older widowers.

Jones (1987) in discussing the reasons for the increased morbidity and mortality proposed that there may be other underlying mechanisms operating in addition to the stressful life event of bereavement. These included homogamy (which is the tendency of spouses to have similar physical and mental characteristics), a common marital environment, the simultaneous death of husband and wife (especially in a single accident or violent incident), the loss of spousal support in respect of nursing or other care with a reduction in motivation, a less adequate diet, increased poverty or changes in social networks, and the postponement of death during illness of the spouse, especially where one spouse is caring for another spouse during a terminal illness.

Chapter 3

UNDERSTANDING GRIEF: THEORETICAL ASPECTS

Human beings attempt to make sense of their world and the people around them. They attempt to fit different physical and psychological phenomena into their cognitive schemata, and to gain mastery over them by identifying, labelling, hypothesising, manipulating, and observing the consequences. Parkes (1988) has suggested that the internal world or the "assumptive world" of the individual, which is based on previous experience, is being constantly matched against incoming sensory data in order to orient, recognise what is happening, and plan behavior accordingly. Understanding loss and its reactions and implications, both in the individual and in others, takes up much of the energy and time of the "assumptive world."

Loss is a universal experience, often painful, which has important physical and psychological repercussions and sometimes threatens the basis of existence. The loss of self, annihilation, and death pose dilemmas and core anxiety which have been addressed by existential philosophers and therapists such as Yalom (1980).

Coming to terms with loss may be a powerful activator of growth. Fleming (1963) regarded partial and temporary separations from libidinal objects as experiences which from birth promote activation of adaptive mechanisms of the ego. He compared this process with the work of mourning. Smith (1971) suggested that the experience of loss may help to provide the establishment of boundaries.

Grieving may be viewed as an automatic process which follows loss and accompanies and expedites a return to normal functioning.

The outward manifestations of grief may be understood simply as a posture which elicits care from the social network. The communication of distress attracts attention and support from those around. The crying and verbal and cognitive manifestations of grief may be a cathartic process, in which release of tension is achieved by an outward expression

13

of emotion. However, in many situations of grief, an abreaction or catharsis of emotion is a temporary phenomenon which may have no long-term benefits or effects, unless there has been a change in attitude and behavior and some adaptation. Freud (1957) recognised the repetitive and protracted nature of the grief process and attempted to understand it in terms of a gradual letting go of libidinal bonds through a process which he regarded as the work of mourning.

All the approaches and models discussed below attempt to provide a framework for understanding grief. Some may be used to predict grief responses in particular subgroups, others focus on the natural history of intrapsychic or interpersonal processes, and others examine biological and physical aspects of grief. The application of theory in the management of grief, particularly in abnormal reactions, is not always so obvious.

Aberbach (1987) compared the processes occurring in mysticism and grief, including withdrawal, yearning and searching, depression and despair, finding, transformation, and a return to a normal social life. It was suggested that the climactic stage of the mystical process, which consisted of the perception of a divine presence, had a parallel in the grief process, in which identification or a sense of union with the lost person occurred. Mysticism could sometimes be used as an outlet for the expression of grief.

Mathers (1974) proposed that some kinds of critical changes in a person's life experience brought about a change in the sense of identity which is not subjectively recognised or acknowledged until between one and two years after the critical event. This "gestation" period appeared to follow major life changes, educational programs, or psychotherapy. It does seem to take from one to two years, following a bereavement from a close attachment figure, to emerge with a free sense of identity, and an ability to engage more fully again in life.

THE INTERNAL DYNAMICS OF GRIEVING

"Mourning" is the term which is often preferred by psychoanalytical writers to refer to the psychological and intrapersonal processes which take place after bereavement.

Freud (1957) drew attention to intrapsychic processes in his work on mourning and melancholia. He drew parallels between mourning, focussing on the psychology of grieving, and melancholia, which appeared to include some severe depressive conditions. A theoretical model was produced which explained some of the symptoms of melancholia and also those found in the grieving person.

The symptoms of mourning, which included a profoundly painful dejection, cessation of interest in the outside world, loss of the capacity to love and an inhibition of all activity were thought to be identical to those found in melancholia, apart from the frequent emergence of feelings of self-reproach which could reach delusional intensity in melancholia. While melancholia could arise following an observable loss or bereavement, some states of melancholia appeared to arise without any such precipitant and it was postulated that in these cases there had been an earlier loss in which the object had been introjected at an unconscious level and was now being severely reprimanded by a part of the functioning self, with resulting self reproach and self-denigration. This can be seen to reflect the ambivalence in relationships in which a libidinal attachment is accompanied by destructive feelings.

Overall, the process of mourning was seen to involve an active but painful process in which the bereaved person was required to break libidinal ties with the lost object, one by one, by a process of recall and review of memories and affects of the deceased, in order to have energy available again to invest in a new relationship. The dilemma was highlighted in which the lost object was both clung to but in keeping with reality testing had to be painfully and reluctantly given up.

These formulations have been useful in stimulating an interest in intrapsychic processes and the origins of guilt and drawing attention to the parallel processes which occur in grief and in depressive disorders. The suggestion that lowered self-esteem and self-reproach never occur in a normal grief reaction has been questioned by Parkes (1980) and Krupp (1969). However, the extremes of self-denigration and persisting low self-esteem are not seen in normal grief.

The rapidity with which the grossly lowered self-esteem and guilty self-reproach of the melancholic are removed or relieved by modern antidepressant treatments are suggestive of abnormalities of neurochemical functioning in these disorders. In remission, or following such treatment, the melancholic is no longer preoccupied with his worthlessness and is no longer attacking himself in word or deed, which leads to the question of what has happened to the attacks on his internalised objects.

Deutsch (1937) examined the absence of expressions of grief which occurred following some bereavements and considered this a defensive attempt of the ego to preserve itself in the face of overwhelming anxiety.

The death of a libidinal object is experienced as separation from a needed source of supply, which threatens the self. The more immature the ego, the more needed is the object so that more intense anxiety will be experienced as a result of the loss. Ambivalence and unneutralised aggression present in the preloss relationship were regarded as important in determining the quantity of stress.

Fleming (1963) regarded the defences of repression and a denial of perceptual reality accompanied by a fantasied continuation of the lost relationship as being normal in the early stages of a mourning process, but, when prolonged, considered that they absorbed the energy necessary for growth and the establishment of new relationships.

Krupp (1965) described identification as a mechanism in mourning in which introjection of the lost object occurred together with an alteration in the self, so that the individual takes on observable qualities and characteristics of the deceased. He described four types of internalisation mechanisms including depressive introjection and symptomatic, personality, and constructive identifications. Depressive introjection occurred in normal mourning. Its absence indicated pathology. Symptomatic identifications included those in which symptoms of the deceased developed, such as anxiety attacks, muscle weakness, nausea, vomiting, or pain symptoms, and functioned simultaneously to bring back the loved one and to inflict self-punishment for having wished the other's death. Personality identifications occurred frequently under stress and consisted of the adoption of the mannerisms and characteristics of the deceased. Constructive identifications occurred following the depressive period when the activities and interests of the deceased were sometimes adopted. The energy previously discharged towards the deceased was redirected onto an internalised object representation of that person, which could reactivate earlier demands and frustrations and result in overinvolvement with the internal object. This latter process was termed hypercathexis.

Many individuals cope with loss by retaining a strongly held memento or memory of that loss or by incorporating the lost person into their personality, in the manner suggested above. Lopata (1986) suggested that part of the grieving process is the reconstruction of the memory about life before the death and that reliving the past brings it into the present.

Lampl de Groot (1983) considered that three factors which influenced the course of mourning included the person's ability to master unconscious guilt feelings and the associated need for punishment due to repressed infantile death wishes towards the deceased, the overcoming of unconscious triumph over the deceased, with manifestations of survivor guilt, and a capacity to sublimate destructive impulses into constructive activities.

Survivor guilt may be implicated in a negative therapeutic reaction as described by Nightingale (1989) when guilt feelings emerge after encouraging experiences have occurred in therapy.

Smith (1971) discussed the development of depression as a defence against grieving and suggested that it was the appearance of the capacity to grieve without euphoria and without mania which signalled the authentic overcoming of depression.

Idealisation of the deceased spouse has been measured in the "sanctification" scores described by Lopata (1986). Many ethnically identified white widows scored higher than nonwhite widows. It was thought that the attitudes associated with sanctification removed from the deceased husband mortal sentiments such as jealousy or tendency to be critical of the wife, reduced feelings of unworthiness in the widow and enabled the past to be constructed as unusually pleasant. However, associates who knew the husband could be alienated if they remembered the husband very differently. Future relationships of the widow with living men could be jeopardised if they had to compete against an idealised man.

One potential result of loss may be the attempted substitution of the lost object. This may result in falling in love soon after a bereavement which was described by Bak (1973). This could be maladaptive if the loss is thereby denied, grief avoided or properties of the deceased are incorrectly assigned to the substitute.

Volkan (1972) described the adoption and use of inanimate objects in pathological mourning, which he termed "linking objects." These were objects which had been worn by the deceased, those which were an extension of the body, like a camera, those with realistic or symbolic resemblance to the deceased, such as a photo, or objects at hand when the news of the death came, thus becoming objects of the "last moment." The linking object had a dual role, in that an impulse to destroy it and an impulse to preserve it could be maintained externally in a dynamic conflict. There was often a conflict between a desire to see it and a desire to keep it out of sight but knowledge of the whereabouts of the objects was very important. It served as an instrument for the control of expression of anger arising from separation panic. Memorials, which are discussed in Chapter 8, may take on some attributes of linking objects.

ATTACHMENT THEORY

Bowlby (1980) developed attachment theory which incorporated psychoanalytical and ethological ideas, but also stressed the importance of interpersonal processes. Attachment theory is of importance in understanding grief reactions more fully. Central to its formulations are an examination of phenomena subsequent to separation or loss in childhood, personality development, and the consequences of loss in adulthood.

Attachment behavior was thought to have survival value for many species. The attachment figure, such as the mother, provided a secure base from which the individual could explore the environment and could retreat to if threatened. Separation from the attachment figure could be accompanied by physical danger and be biologically disadvantageous. Separation from the attachment figure in the young child was observed to be followed by a sequence of protest, with tears and anger, and then by quiet, despairing preoccupation, which sometimes alternated with a phase of hope and yearning. If reunion with the attachment figure occurred, the child was initially unresponsive, which was eventually replaced by an intense show of emotion, with clinging behavior, and the development of rage and anxiety whenever the mother briefly left the child.

Grief in the adult was conceptualised as a form of separation anxiety that resulted from the disruption of an attachment bond through loss. The searching behavior or anger which arose following bereavement could be viewed as an automatic reaction to loss, which served in the small child to reestablish union with the lost person.

Bowlby considered that the development of pathological grief reactions depended on childhood experiences which led to three disordered forms of attachment, including anxious attachment, compulsive self-reliance, and compulsive care giving. Individuals who developed anxious attachment to parents were particularly likely to be subsequently insecurely attached to and overdependent on their marriage partners. Chronic grief reactions were likely to develop following spousal bereavement. The compulsively self reliant or "pseudo independent" individuals were likely to deny their loss, with delay in onset of their grief reactions. Compulsive care givers were also thought to develop abnormalities of grieving.

ATTACHMENT AND LOSS IN ADULTS

Weiss (1988) utilised and extended the above theory to examine grief in adults further. He termed those relationships whose loss triggers grief with severe and persisting distress as "relationships of attachment," which usually comprise pair-bond relationships, parental attachments to children, transference relationships to helpers or persisting childlike attachments to parents. Those relationships whose loss did not trigger such profound grief were termed relationships of community and comprised those of friends, colleagues, or adult siblings living in different households.

Weiss drew attention to features of attachment behavior, which if aroused and frustrated, result in the manifestations of grief. It was pointed out that attachment behavior, which was security fostering, was displayed under conditions of threat and was not under conscious control. Attachments to particular figures tended to persist over time, did not wane through habituation, and persisted even if the attachment figure was abusive or neglecting.

In the movement towards recovery from or adaptation to grief, three processes were described, of cognitive acceptance, emotional acceptance and identity change. The cognitive acceptance involved the individual developing a satisfactory account of the causes of the loss event. The emotional acceptance involved a neutralisation of the pain of memories and associations, while an identity change consisted of the connection to the attachment figure being viewed as part of a past self rather than a present self.

He considered that failure to recover could be characterised by chronicity or "compartmentalisation" in which feelings of loss were fended off and energy was given to weakening the stimulus value of any observation or memory that might trigger off an awareness of the loss. It differed from repression or denial in that there was no refusal to recognise reality, only a refusal to attend to it. It was suggested that the resulting guardedness could generalise and impoverish the emotional life and prevent the establishment of new emotional relationships.

LATENT SELF-IMAGES AND GRIEF

Horowitz et al. (1980) have hypothesised that pathological grief is an intensification of normal grief in individuals who have latent images of themselves as bad, incompetent, or hurtful. These negative images, which had been held in check by the existence of a close relationship with another individual were reactivated following the death of that person. Self-concepts that appeared to complicate grieving included feeling too weak to function without the deceased (resulting in overwhelming instead of tolerable sadness), considering oneself hostile and somehow responsible for the death (leading to intensified guilt), and feeling damaged or defective (leading to a sense of emptiness and apathy).

BEHAVIORAL AND COGNITIVE MODELS

Stroebe et al. (1987) have drawn attention to the focus of behavioral theory on depression, rather than grief, but suggest that following bereavement many rewards are no longer available while others have lost their reinforcing quality. The extinction of a repertoire of reinforcements and responses, which is painful and frustrating for rats trained in a Skinner box, is even more painful for the bereaved spouse. The reduction of response-contingent positive reinforcement and a related increase in aversive events could serve as an unconditioned stimulus for feelings of sadness, fatigue, and somatic symptoms which are found in grief. In some individuals the grieving posture may be maintained by reinforcement from the social network which continues granting privileges or rewards to the bereaved individual over a prolonged period.

Behavioral theory appears to have some practical implications in addressing the prolonged avoidance behavior which some individuals demonstrate in the course of pathological grief reactions and which may be overcome by guided mourning techniques as described by Mawson et al. (1981).

Cognitive therapy, which applies some aspects of behavioral theory to the cognitive processes, has shown considerable promise in the treatment of depressive disorders. Beck (1981) has emphasised the link between distorted and repetitive trains of thought and their effect on mood, and has attempted to modify those thoughts which are negative, self-defeating, or clearly inconsistent with good social functioning. The isolated, bereaved individual is more likely to continue to have unmodified patterns of grief, which may include some negative cognitive self appraisals. Modifying, interrupting or reshaping these thought processes may require the presence and input of other individuals.

SOCIAL MODELS

The focus of many researchers has extended to an examination of the social network of the bereaved. It is frequently noted that the isolated bereaved individual is at a greater risk of developing a range of complications. Brown et al. (1978) have demonstrated that social support is protective against the deleterious effects of critical life events. Man is a social being and is dependent for physical and emotional supplies on others. The loss of a more intensive or closer relationship consequently creates a greater reaction which is manifested in the overall picture of grief.

Stroebe et al. (1987) have proposed a "deficit model" following loss of a partner in which losses of instrumental and emotional support and loss of social identity act as stressors which modify the grief process. Both intrapersonal resources (a nonneurotic personality) and interpersonal resources (social support) could mitigate the extremes of grief. Those with the greatest losses or least coping sources would predictably be at greatest risk. The importance of social support was stressed in minimising adverse outcomes.

Parkes (1988) also examined the magnitude of losses which could arise following the loss of a spouse. The possible losses which could occur included those of a sexual partner, protection from danger, reassurance of worth, employment, companionship, income, recreational partner, status, expectations, self-confidence, home, being a parent, and many others. However, the loss of a spouse could also produce relief from responsibilities, entitlement to the care of others, sympathy from others, attributions of heroism, financial gains, and freedom to realise potentials that had been inhibited.

Parkes (1988) defined a psychosocial transition (PST) as a dangerous life event that:

a) required people to undertake a major revision of their assumptions about the world
b) were lasting in their implications rather than transient
c) took place over a relatively short time period.

He suggested that the internal world or "assumptive world" of the individual is required to change during the course of a PST, that each PST is regarded as a "job of work" in order to adapt to the requirements of the real world and that pain and anxiety were often associated. The outcome of a PST appeared to be related to the magnitude of the PST, the extent to which it had been correctly anticipated and the supports and opportunities available. Following the death of a loved person it was suggested that a characteristic emotion was evoked which was largely independent of the magnitude of the resulting life change.

It seems likely that a core of grief symptoms is manifested by many bereaved individuals, but these are modified by the social support and input available. Additional impairments or pathology and a prolonged difficulty in adaptation may be experienced by individuals who have been subjected to multiple losses or whose internal coping resources are inadequate.

Death and loss often occur in family situations, in which the bereaved partner is part of a family system, which tends to resist change. Role reallocation may take time and family dynamics may become disturbed until a new homeostasis has been established. Dysfunctional families may demonstrate pathological reactions to grief demonstrating denial, chronic mourning, or a myth or pretence of the old status quo and a continued fantasy of survival of the deceased member.

Symbolic interaction theory (see Marris, 1974) regards social interaction as a basis for defining events, feelings, and meanings which are of great importance in the development of a personal sense of stability. Loss of a person consequently causes instability which may result in a bereaved person searching for potential sources of meaning in different venues or attaching increased importance to possessions to the extent that the inheritance of property can become a source of dispute.

REMINDER THEORY

Rosenblatt (1983) suggested the notion that specific stimuli set off memories and behavior patterns that are linked to the deceased. The grieving process is thereby accelerated if the bereaved is in contact with the environment in which the deceased lived. Grieving is seen as an intermittent process which is not continuous. People may need to back away from their grief for some of the time and adopt strategies of emotional control, which may be related to social or subsistence demands. Cognitive reminders may then trigger off further mourning. This was illustrated in an examination of nineteenth century diarists who experienced losses by separation and death.

SOCIAL RELATIONSHIPS AS BIOLOGICAL REGULATORS

The notion that components of the grief process may be independent of each other and altered by different physical, social, and psychological cues or their withdrawal is a fascinating one. The acute affective disturbance may be distinguished from chronic background physiological and psychological processes, which may all be differentially influenced by different factors. The understanding of mechanisms by which a social cue or the presence of another person can have such a profound effect on the biology of a person would help to illuminate the biology of grief.

Hofer (1984) attempted to integrate ideas on biological rhythms, biological regulators (and their withdrawal), and grief in an imaginative way. He discussed biological regulators in animal models. In rats, physical contact, body warmth, olfaction, maternal milk, and feeding had differential influence on infant behavior, activity levels, metabolism, heart rate and sleep patterns. He suggested that biologic regulators may constitute an early stage in the development of psychologic regulators within early social interactions as infants get older and species evolve.

He drew attention to the possibility that the acute and chronic phases of the reaction to early maternal separation can be affected differentially and may be independent processes, as demonstrated in infant bonnet macaque monkeys which became more depressed and despairing during the second week of separation if the previous mother-infant relationship had been tense as a result of the mother being required to forage for food.

He pointed out that in adult animals and humans, homeostatic regulatory systems remain under environmental control to a certain degree as demonstrated by young women who live together for a time who develop synchrony in their menstrual cycles. The question was then posed whether some of the changes that follow human bereavement result from withdrawal of specific sensorimotor regulators hidden within the complex interactions of the relationship that has ended. A comparison of the symptoms occurring after sensory deprivation experiments in humans and the chronic symptoms occurring in bereavement was made to support this notion.

In discussing biological rhythms which require synchronization by environmental events or "Zeitgebers," he proposed that in bereavement of a close partner, a withdrawal of a multitude of "Zeitgebers" occurred including a withdrawal of those sensorimotor cues (e.g., sight, smell, sound, touch of the deceased) which would be expected, and also a possible withdrawal of internal mental representations, which could both have a disrupting effect on the biological clock. The symptoms of disruption of the biological clock, occurring in jet lag, change of work shift or sensory deprivation experiments were compared to those occurring in grief.

However, a closer examination of the symptoms in these conditions reveals a diverse range of psychological symptoms, which differ markedly in intensity. Perhaps the most prominent symptoms occurring in grief are the changes in mood, with dejection, depression, low self-esteem, self-reproach, yearning, and the powerful images and recollections of the deceased, which do not occur especially in the jet lag, change of work shift or sensory deprivation experiments. Symptoms such as decreased concentration, malaise, appetitive and sleep disturbances are common in many mental and physical illnesses and occur following non specific stressors which are not necessarily closely linked with an alteration in circadian rhythms. If similar changes in neurophysiological and endocrine functioning could be demonstrated in grief and the disorders thought to be associated with an alteration in biological rhythms, and specific "Zeitgebers" could be shown to alter these parameters, the above theories would become more plausible.

A THEORY ON THE FUNCTIONS OF MEMORY REVIEW OF THE DECEASED

The persistent recall of memories of the deceased which occurs in the first few months of grieving, which may be triggered off by environmental cues, anniversaries or other events, is a phenomenon which deserves further consideration. These memories cover many details of the deceased, are repetitive and are only partially under voluntary control.

This memory review may serve to establish the reality of the situation (the deceased is alive in memory, but not externally), may be guilt-relieving (paying homage to the deceased), may be part of the work of mourning as described by Freud (1957), in which libidinal ties to the internalised object are broken one by one or may serve to desensitise the individual to the pain of loss, as each time the memory of the deceased occurs, there is less negative affect associated.

A function of this memory review which has not been previously considered is that the loss of an object can be minimised or counteracted by establishing a stronger or more concrete memory of that person, which is then available when the bereaved wishes for comfort. The memory may be strengthened (and made clearer) by many repetitions in the context of some heightening of emotional arousal. There is a natural movement by human beings to minimise loss, and this is a cognitive means of achieving this. Parkes (1980) pointed out that unlike most other psychological features of grieving, the memory of the dead person tends to increase in the course of the first year of bereavement and quoted C.S. Lewis who remembered his wife best when he was mourning her least.

It is of interest that many individuals who experience a strong sense of presence of the deceased or who experience illusions or hallucinatory-type phenomena are comforted by these experiences. The ability to cognitively recollect the deceased in a vivid manner many years after bereavement may also be a source of comfort.

CONCLUSIONS

Theories of grief have developed considerably since Freud wrote "Melancholia and Mourning" in 1917 in which intrapsychic mechanisms were proposed and parallels drawn between grief and depressive disorders. Bowlby (1980) has derived some of his ideas from Freud, but incorporated ethological factors, drawn attention to the species-survival value of grief, which may be observed in nonhuman species following loss, and has highlighted the reactions of infants and children to separation and loss. Psychosocial theories have paid more attention to the social context of grief, both in impact and repercussions. Behavioral and cognitive theories have been of value in devising some treatment strategies in states of abnormal grieving.

The interplay of biological parameters, social relationships and grief as proposed by Hofer (1984) opens exciting possibilities for further research utilising animal prototypes and humans.

Chapter 4

BIOLOGICAL ASPECTS OF GRIEF

THE PHYSIOLOGY OF BEREAVEMENT

The observable physical changes which accompany bereavement, including agitation, crying, tears, sighing respiration, alterations in sleep pattern, appetitive changes, and alterations in mental state are suggestive of underlying physiological changes.

Sadness and grief are often accompanied by enhanced sympathetic responses. Averill (1969) demonstrated increased sympathetic activity during both sadness and mirth provoking films in male subjects. Increased electrodermal activity and increased heart rate and particularly blood pressure were more prominent in the sadness than mirth provoking films.

Hirsch et al. (1984) suggested that the acute waves of distress in grief could be further investigated using tests of respiratory control, blood gases, cardiovascular function, and energy metabolism, while the chronic disturbance could be investigated by examining circadian rhythms of body temperature, physical activity, cardiac rate, and urinary output.

The apparent increase in physical ill health following bereavement may be mediated through changes in immunological or endocrine functioning. Some bereaved individuals may neglect themselves and pay insufficient attention to nutrition, hygiene or exercise, consume more alcohol or tobacco, or engage in risk-taking activities which may jeopardise their health.

A vulnerability to physical ill health may arise from alterations in the status of the immune system, which could lead to an increased susceptibility to infection or malignancy. Sudden cardiac crises which are associated with bereavement may be mediated by changes in autonomic arousal and in the levels of circulating catecholamines.

THE IMMUNE SYSTEM AND BEREAVEMENT

The function of the immune system in bereavement has been studied by Bartrop et al. (1977) and Schleifer et al. (1983). Bereaved individuals were found to have an impaired function of T-lymphocytes which was not a concomitant of a reduction in circulating T-cells or of changes in adrenal or thyroid hormones.

Bartrop et al. (1977) demonstrated a significantly reduced lymphocyte response to mitogens in spouses two months postbereavement compared with control subjects, while Schleifer et al. (1983) found that a depression of lymphocyte response did not occur prebereavement in men whose wives had terminal breast cancer, but only after bereavement.

Irwin et al. (1987) discussed the findings that depressive symptoms are accompanied by a reduction in natural killer cell (N.K.) activity and attempted to explore this in bereaved women who may experience significant depressive symptoms. It was concluded that although depressive symptoms may possibly mediate immunologic changes during bereavement, the processes that modulate the immune system and link bereavement, changes in central nervous system activity and immune function remain unknown. It was considered that altered N.K. activity during both anticipatory and actual bereavement could not be explained solely on the basis of increased cortisol production.

The above research indicates some alterations in the functioning of the immune system, but it is unclear whether the in vitro tests of immune function are related to an increased vulnerability to infection in the clinical setting. Further research which directly measures immune function in human beings in vivo is required to elucidate these matters.

THE ENDOCRINE SYSTEM AND BEREAVEMENT

Anticipation of a loss or an actual loss may be accompanied by an activation of the hypothalamic pituitary adrenal axis and the sympathetic nervous system, with activation of the adrenal cortex and medulla.

Wolff et al. (1964) examined the adrenocortical function in the parents of children dying of leukemia and found a relationship between urinary levels of 17 hydroxycorticosteroids (17-O.H.C.S.) and the effectiveness of psychological defenses, with more effective defenses being associated with lower 17-O.H.C.S. levels. The longitudinal course of psychological distress may be more predictive of adrenocortical activity than isolated levels of distress (Jacobs et al., 1986).

It is possible that the immediate intense waves of distress in bereavement are accompanied by sympathetic and adrenal medullary overactivity, while chronic distress is accompanied by alterations in adrenocortical functioning.

Adrenocortical activity is related to alterations in immune function, while an increase in circulating catecholamines may be related to a sudden cardiac death, cardiac arrhythmias, myocardial infarction, and congestive cardiac failure, which would be particularly pronounced in those patients with preexisting cardiovascular disease (Hirsch et al., 1984).

ANIMAL MODELS OF BEREAVEMENT

Bowlby (1961) has drawn attention to the reaction of members of lower species such as the jackdaw, goose, dog, orangutan and chimpanzee to protest at the loss of a loved object and to do all in their power to seek and recover it, which may be accompanied by hostility, withdrawal, apathy, and restlessness. These reactions may be compared to the grief reaction in humans, and have implications for the survival of the individual and the species. These reactions would be of particular importance in the immature and more vulnerable animals and in members of a species which are highly dependent on social support for functioning.

Laudenslager (1988) and Hirsch et al. (1984) discussed the utility of animal models of bereavement in order to clarify the biological processes occurring in human bereavement.

Hirsch et al. (1984) drew attention to the striking similarities in chronic biological responses to early separation between monkeys and rats, with a reduction in rapid eye movement sleep with insomnia, a lowering of cardiac rate, a thermoregulatory disturbance with decrease of core temperature and a decrease in immune competence.

Laudenslager (1988) reviewed studies of the responses of infant monkeys to loss and discussed the behavioral, autonomic, endocrine, and immune responses which occurred. The behavioral responses in infant monkeys separated from the mother included stages of protest-despair followed by withdrawal, which could be compared with those occurring in the human infant. Autonomic responses, including alterations in heart rate and arrhythmias, changes in sleep pattern and in circadian rhythms of body temperature and heart rate bore some resemblance to those occurring in children briefly separated from the mother during birth of a sibling. Endocrine changes involving the hypothalamic-pituitary-adrenal (H.P.A.) axis were noted in some monkey studies and were compared to increased urinary cortisol levels reflecting H.P.A. activity which have been observed in one year human infants separated from mother for one hour. The immunological changes in the infant monkey were thought to parallel those found in recently bereaved adult humans. Attention was drawn to differences occurring between squirrel and pig-tail monkeys. The presence of familiar others or the home cage environment had an ameliorating effect in restoring the antibody response in maternally separated squirrel monkeys, which did not occur in pigtail monkeys.

However, because of the differences between mammalian species, these animal models can only be suggestive of physiological mechanisms in humans. It is important to distinguish different types of loss, which may include complete or partial loss of mother, with loss of peers or of familiar environment as additional variables. The responses at different ages or at different levels of maturity, the relationship preceding the loss and ameliorating factors following the loss may all require careful assessment in the animal models studied. It is still open to speculation whether some of the physiological changes following the above losses represent a reaction to a nonspecific stress rather than comprising a specific "bereavement syndrome."

Chapter 5

PATHOLOGICAL LAUGHING AND CRYING

Pathological laughing and crying are discussed together, as there may be underlying cerebral pathology in common.

Laughing and crying are both human behaviors which are frequent and from which the observer makes inferences about the underlying emotional state. It is often assumed that spontaneous laughter reflects an underlying joy, euphoria, or appreciation of a good joke, while crying and tears reflect sadness, hurt, or a sense of loss, but this is not always the situation when there is an underlying mental illness or neuropathological syndrome. Abnormalities of spontaneous laughing and crying occur in terms of precipitants, propagation and underlying psychological processes and are found in certain psychiatric and neurological disorders which are discussed below.

Laughing and crying are complex behaviors involving the coordination of facial and respiratory muscles, with the production of characteristic sounds and movements. These behaviors are thought to be under the dual control of voluntary and involuntary neurological mechanisms (Wilson, 1924).

Crying is ontogenetically earlier than laughter in the infant and it has been suggested that it is a more primitive response (Poeck, 1969), although both laughter and crying involve similar areas of the central nervous system and motor structures. Wilson (1924) postulated a centre linking the seventh nerve nucleus in the pons with the motor nucleus of the tenth nerve in the medulla and with phrenic nuclei in the upper cervical cord, and an integrative centre in the mesial thalamus, hypothalamus, and subthalamus, which was under dual control, both voluntary and involuntary. The limbic system is thought to be involved in laughing and crying (Black, 1982), and may be associated with the screening of incoming stimuli for their emotional importance to the organism, generating positive and negative emotional responses and activating pathways producing coordinated motor responses for emotional expression. A postulated laughing centre in the hypothalamus and other biological, psychological, and social aspects of humor and laughter are discussed in detail elsewhere (Haig, 1988; McGhee and Goldstein, 1983). It is possible that a similar coordinating centre may be involved in the actions of crying.

DEFINING PATHOLOGICAL LAUGHING AND CRYING

A wide range of conditions with an identifiable underlying organic basis and other conditions such as the functional psychoses and hysteria may be associated with abnormalities of laughing and crying. Wilson (1924) included conditions with focal organic pathology in his consideration of exaggerated or uncontrollable laughing or crying, but excluded hysteria and also some chronic neurological disorders in which irritability and tearfulness were common.

Poeck (1969) also took a narrower view of pathological laughing and crying, excluding those conditions in which there appeared to be a disorder of the emotions underlying the facial manifestations. He described four criteria characterising pathological laughing and crying which included a response to non-specific stimuli, an absence of a similarly oriented change in affect or the lack of a relationship between affective change and the observed expressions and an absence of a corresponding change in mood lasting beyond the actual laughing or crying including a lack of relief after such an expression of mood. He considered the third criterion to be the most important.

Black (1984) restricted his review to laughter, but took a wider view in his definition and classification. Duchowny (1983) defined pathological laughter as an abnormal behavioral response that superficially resembles natural laughter, but differs by virtue of abnormalities of motor patterns, emotional experience, or appropriateness of social context. Utilising this definition, but applying it to both laughing and crying, it is possible to describe four broad categories which include inappropriate, excessive, forced laughing and crying, and gelastic epilepsy. From the viewpoint of the psychiatrist, this classification corresponds with the order of frequency in which these conditions would be encountered in practice. The following classification is based on a consideration of both the form, and aetiology involved:

1. INAPPROPRIATE LAUGHING AND CRYING

These are the expressions which would conventionally be linked with schizophrenia, conversion disorders or histrionic personality disorders.

In the disorganised schizophrenic, split expressions of laughter, joy, and sorrow were described by Bleuler (1924) as "parathymia." He stated that "a particularly frequent form of parathymia is represented by unprovoked or inappropriate bursts of laughter." Kraepelin (1919) had drawn attention to "silly laughter," which was unrestrained, unprovoked, and without emotional significance as a symptom of dementia praecox.

Both tears and laughter may appear in rapid succession in the schizophrenic with a hebephrenic picture and do not always appear to be closely related to the underlying emotional state and are often inappropriate to the social environment. The displays of emotion may be clearly inappropriate, as evidenced by a schizophrenic girl, who alternated between laughter and crying in rapid succession. She experienced congruent emotions of joy or sadness while laughing or crying, but could not give any reason why her mood fluctuated rapidly between these extremes. Humor in normals often arises as a response to incongruity and its resolution (Haig, 1988), and it may be that in some schizophrenics incongruous thoughts and perceptions are processed utilising a humor response. Laughter may also arise as a habitual response to conceal or reduce anxiety, and this may also occur in schizophrenics with increased levels of anxiety. The cynical or "hollow" laughter occurring in some schizophrenics may reflect underlying delusional or hallucinatory phenomena.

The individual with a histrionic personality may manifest overt emotions which are both extreme and inappropriate. "Hysterical" laughter or crying may occur in normal individuals following massive psychological trauma, and could be regarded as a tension release mechanism or, if inappropriate, as a form of denial.

Group hysterical laughter has been described. The most dramatic case in the literature, described by Bean (1967), commenced in an African convent school, where contagious laughter caused the closure of fourteen schools, and spread in an epidemic fashion to the local community.

In some schizophrenic and hysterical forms of inappropriate laughing and crying, it seems that there is a functional impairment of cortical control over the motor centres responsible for these behaviors, with an additional dissociation between these centres and the limbic system which is responsible for emotional tone and experience.

2. EXCESSIVE LAUGHING AND CRYING

These are the conditions in which there is an increase in emotional lability and an apparent failure in inhibitory mechanisms, often as a result of organic factors. At its most extreme, following frontal lobe syndromes or tertiary syphilis, patient exhibited "Witzelsucht," a prankish joking or punning, or "moria," a childish excitement (Lishman, 1978). The accompanying fatuous euphoria indicated that other listeners did not share the euphoria nor did they appreciate the humor. Differing degrees of excessive laughing and crying occurs in many of the organic mood disorders, organic personality syndromes, substance use disorders or intoxication with substances ranging from alcohol to nitrous oxide. The underlying mood may correspond grossly to the outward display of emotion, as in the "maudlin drunk" who feels morose in addition to shedding tears. In many of these conditions, a focal neurological impairment is not evident but a generalised cerebral dysfunction may be inferred.

In severe physical and mental fatigue, excessive laughing and crying may occur.

In the mood disorders, excessive laughing or crying may occur in manic or depressive states respectively, but these behaviors appear to be related to a pathological alteration of mood, without the identifiable organic pathology which appears in the above conditions.

3. FORCED LAUGHING AND CRYING

In these conditions, there is an involuntary outburst of explosive, self-sustained laughing or crying, following a nonspecific or inappropriate stimulus, such as being touched by the bed clothes, seeing someone yawn, or when being spoken to. This picture is sometimes found following pseudobulbar palsies after multiple infarcts in the basal brain region, or in pontobulbar palsies associated with amyotrophic lateral sclerosis, although it may also occur in a variety of disorders such as Parkinson's disease, multiple sclerosis, and many multifocal cerebral diseases. Forced or excessive laughter has developed in psychotic patients who were treated with bilateral prefrontal lobotomies (Kramer, 1954).

Gaze-induced pathological laughter in a patient with an extramedullary brainstem tumour was described by Leopold (1977).

The laughter may be inappropriate to the underlying emotion which often consists of embarrassment or distress, while the underlying emotion in forced crying often does not consist of sadness, although Kinnier Wilson suggested that the laughing or crying are not entirely divorced from the underlying emotional state.

Forced laughing may switch into crying. Wilson (1924) referred to an account by Brissaud of a patient with "pleurer spasmodique" who was in a bed next to a patient with "rire spasmodique." The latter patient roared with laughter at the weeping of the former, leading on occasion to the first to change his weeping to an equally phenomenal laughter, which illustrates the lability and incongruence of the emotional expression in some of these cases. Following the laughing or crying, the patient does not experience the cathartic relief which normally comes from such expressions.

These conditions usually result from bilateral interruption of descending voluntary motor pathways which normally inhibit the subcortical centres mediating "emotional" motor responses. Poeck (1969) suggested that lesions at the following levels of the pyramidal and extrapyramidal pathways could be responsible:

a. internal capsule with involvement of basal ganglia;
b. substantia nigra;
c. cerebral peduncles and caudal hypothalamus;
d. bilateral lesions of the pyramidal tracts along with the extrapyramidal fibres that accompany them.

4. GELASTIC EPILEPSY

This is part of an epileptic phenomenon in which laughter (or, less frequently, crying) appears, usually with loss of consciousness, other convulsive motor change, abnormalities of eye movements, and autonomic disturbances.

The incidence is less than 0.32 percent of epileptics. It may arise from lesions of the frontal and temporal lobes as well as from subcortical structures including the hypothalamus. Variable EEG changes occur. It may arise in childhood and be associated with precocious puberty, both disorders being associated with pathology in the posterior hypothalamus (Williams et al., 1980). Duchowny (1983) divided gelastic seizures into hypothalamic and limbic. Hypothalamic attacks consisted of brief episodes of elementary laughter, with loss of consciousness and retrograde amnesia for the event, whereas limbic seizures were more variable and showed diverse behavioral manifestations and a variety of emotional sensations.

Cursive epilepsy in which running occurs may coexist with gelastic epilepsy in rare cases (Jandolo et al., 1977).

An unusual case described by Jacome (1980) involved a patient inducing gelastic epilepsy by hyperextending his back, which was also accompanied by an intense sexual feeling. Occasionally seizures commence in neonates (Sher et al., 1976) which suggests that the brain substrates for laughter are functional at birth (Duchowny, 1983).

Other exotic disorders which occasionally give rise to pathological laughing include "fou rire prodromique," a continuous laughing which presages an apoplectic event (and is usually terminal), kuru, a rare but fatal subacute degenerative disease of New Guinea tribesmen, which may be associated with cannibalism, and the "happy puppet syndrome," in which mental retardation, microcephaly, and facial abnormalities occur in conjunction with puppet-like arm movements and frequent laughter (Duchowny 1983). Other disorders of interest include those in which there is a paralysis of voluntary, but not of emotionally mediated, involuntary facial expressions, and vice versa, discussed by Wilson (1924).

CONCLUSIONS

The diverse neurological and psychiatric conditions which have been mentioned above are associated with abnormalities of laughing and crying, which may be inappropriately precipitated, automatically propagated, or lacking congruency with the subjectively experienced emotional tone and cognitive processes. Neurologists who have taken an interest in this area have focussed primarily on identifiable focal organic pathology and have been more interested in forced laughter and gelastic epilepsy. Excessive and inappropriate laughing and crying are seen by psychiatrists but have not been systematically studied. Such a study could further elucidate neurological factors and dissociation of central nervous system functions in mental illness, in addition to illuminating the processes involved in the production of normal laughing and crying.

Certain forms of pathological laughing or crying appear when there has been an impairment of the voluntary motor pathways which normally inhibit subcortical centres responsible for these emotional expressions. (This is clearly the case in forced laughing and crying). Other forms arise when there is an epileptic focus affecting the same subcortical structures while other variants arise in mental illness in which there have not clearly been identified neurological impairments, but in which there may be abnormalities of mood, perception, or cognitive processing.

Laughing or crying do not necessarily indicate joy or sorrow, elevated or depressed mood, or give any indication of normality or psychopathology unless the social environment, the underlying emotional tone and cognitive processes, and any associated underlying abnormality in neuropathology or physiology are all taken into consideration.

The study of these conditions indicates neurological pathways which are involved in the normal production of laughing and crying and are activated during grieving.

In addition to these pathways, emotional arousal, which is prominent during grief or states of sadness, involves activation of the limbic system, which consists of the hypothalamus, anterior thalamic nuclei, cingular gyrus and hippocampus.

A discussion of this (Haig, 1988), in relation to humor, linked sequential and holistic cognitive processing, mood and left-right hemisphere differences. It is probable that major structural or functional abnormalities in these key areas of the brain would likewise effect the experience and course of grief.

Chapter 6

GRIEF AND HUMOR—
THE INTERACTION OF OPPOSITES

And the self same well from which your laughter rises
was oftentimes filled with tears.

The Prophet
Kahil Gibran

The experience and manifestations of grief and of good humor may be viewed as polar opposites but may nevertheless share some features in common and interact in the individual. The sight of the grief stricken child who has lost her doll contrasts vividly with the sight of the same child who is happy and laughing and induces very different responses in the onlooker. It is possible for the child to switch rapidly from tears to laughter given a distraction in an emotionally reassuring environment. The adult likewise may be distracted from moments of despair by humor. In Chapter 5, the rapid transition between laughter and tears was pointed out in certain diseases and conditions effecting the brain.

I compared the features of humor and grief (Haig, 1988) and proposed that the symptoms of grief follow an object loss while those of good humor follow a perceived gain which may take the form of an unexpected meeting with an old friend, a new discovery which contributes to the well-being or self-esteem, or the appreciation of a joke which is accompanied by a sudden resolution of incongruity, which is a cognitive discovery.

The manifestations of good humor, which follows the appreciation of a joke, cartoon, or humorous situation, involve a rapid cognitive appreciation of incongruity. This is followed by laughter with characteristic expiratory vocalisations of a rhythmical, staccato pattern over a five-second period followed by a deep inspiratory gasp over a three-second period with thigh slapping, rocking movements and even some loss of muscular power in the extremes of laughter, which may also be accompanied by lacrimation.

In table 6.1 the features of grief and humor are compared. Culture, gender, age, personality type and educational opportunities all influence the manifestations of both humor and grief.

It can be seen from this table that mood differs markedly between grief and humor, as do the vocalisations, gestures, and effects on social interaction, but the neurological and motor channels are similar and sympathetic arousal occurs in both phenomena. The effects on physical health are of interest, with some evidence of adverse effects on physical health and immunological functioning in grief, with claims that humor enhances health (Cousins, 1979).

TABLE 6.1

The Grief Paradigm	*The Humor Paradigm*
Grief	Good Humor
Characterised by	Characterised by
1. Dysphoria, hopeless despair.	1. Euphoria, buoyant optimism.
2. Sometimes low self esteem.	2. Self-esteem may improve.
3. Characteristic vocalisations—crying, sobbing and tears.	3. Laughter.
4. Similar neuronal motor pathways in grief and humor.	
5. Sympathetic arousal in both grief and humor.	
6. Automatic behavior only partially under voluntary control in both states.	
7. Withdrawal from usual activities.	7. Social reaching out and sharing.
8. Restless, agitated "purposeless" behavior (? searching for lost object).	8. Followed by decisive, goal-oriented behavior.
9. Periodic denial of loss, numbing.	9. Expansion of range of consciousness.
10. Cognitive processing repeatedly of memories of lost object. May begin to achieve resolution over twelve months.	10. Cognitive processing of joke rapid (within seconds). Resolution of incongruity achieved by right cerebral hemisphere.
11. Possible impairment of immunological functioning.	11. Claims that humor is health promoting.
12. Occurs in lower species.	12. Humor and laughter only thought to occur in *Homo sapiens*.
13. Tears and bodily posture signal to those around that support required and individual feels vulnerable.	13. Laughter signals to those around that a discovery has been made and that the individual feels safe.

The individual who is preoccupied with grieving may not be able to appreciate humor and it would be insensitive to suggest the use of humor in this situation. However, humor may be a powerful way of reducing anxiety, transforming pain, so that it loses its intensity without resorting to denial or more primitive defenses, and inducing social cohesion.

Humor may also be a useful way of communicating difficult facts or ideas. Theories of humor have been discussed by Haig (1988) and McGhee et al. (1983).

Humor may spontaneously emerge in the spaces between grief work. It arises following the serious intensity of the funeral ceremony. Families and friends may develop a humorous mode of handling problems including those that involve loss. Jaffe (1976) described how gallows humor helped her and her family to cope with her terminal illness.

An anecdote exists about the minister who was giving a eulogy at a funeral service, about a man who was a rogue of the worst brand and who had no redeeming qualities about him at all. The mourners waited anxiously for the sermon to begin. The minister commenced, with some misgivings, "He wasn't a regular churchgoer and he didn't have any close friends. His wife isn't here because she died of grief and his daughter isn't either—she became a streetwalker after he kicked her out. . . ." Rather than continue with any further faults or deficiencies, the minister groped for something positive to say and finally added, "but compared to his brother, he was a saint."

The "joking-partner" (Haig, 1988) fulfils a formal relationship in many cultures throughout the world. The joking-partner, often a member of another tribe, officiates at the funeral of the partner as well as performing undesirable jobs, such as disposing of the bodies of lepers and suicides and killing abnormal babies. At the funeral ceremony the joking-partner jokes about the deceased and makes suggestive remarks to the widow. This formalised practice may help to reduce tension at the funeral ceremony.

Humor also arises in settings in which health care staff are involved in the stressful areas of caring for very sick or dying patients. This may be useful in reducing anxiety in the staff. The humor may be directly related to patients, or may be directed to situations which arise around the patients and relatives. A traumatic incident may be viewed as humorous in retrospect.

An example of this is that of a matriarchal Lebanese woman who died in the course of a severe illness. Her grown-up daughter who was in the hospital became grief stricken, started wailing, and threw herself on the floor, beating the ground, which was very distressing for other patients and relatives. A staff member knelt down beside her and tried to comfort her. In the meantime, the father appeared with a bucket of water, which he threw over his daughter (and at the staff member). An angry Greek man, a relative of another patient, emerged from another room, accused the Lebanese man of starting wars, and had to be restrained from attacking the Lebanese.

Black humor may be appreciated most by those who have been involved in life threatening situations. Ziv (1984) gives an example of such humor which flourished in Israel during the Yom Kippur War:

> Two soldiers are sitting in a small, cramped barrack.
> "You could easily fit an entire tank division in here," says one.
> "How?"
> "In an ashtray."

This type of humor, also known as gallows humor, may help to defuse tension, but also brings to awareness the horrific nature of a situation.

In the grieving person, it should be cautioned that the use of humor against that individual (humor often has a "butt") should be avoided as it may cause distress.

Chapter 7

MOURNING PRACTICES AND
THE EXPRESSION OF GRIEF

Charon, the mythological Greek ferryman, was always paid a coin to transport the body of a dead person across the River Styx to the other world. There are parallels in the customs of other cultures, including the Chinese, the Slavic, and the Japanese, alluded to by Eisenbruch (1984). The French also used to have a custom of placing a large coin in the mouth of the deceased in order for him to be well received in the next world. Perhaps the payment of a token helps to ease the passage of the bereaved through the early stages of grief as well as speeding the spirit of the deceased towards a mythical afterlife. In this chapter, the relevance of mourning rituals, which may have common core features across cultures, are explored, with a discussion of how they might assist in unlocking grief processes. The development of funeral practices in North America and Australia is reviewed briefly. Finally, the political nature of funerals is discussed.

GRIEF AND RITUAL

The experience and expression of grief by the individual are influenced by the mourning rituals which are practised in a specific culture. There may be a powerful impulse to weep if one is confronted with a sombre funeral ceremony at which mourners are already keening and wailing, even if the deceased is a total stranger. I have discussed the infectious nature of crying and laughing in social situations (Haig, 1988). The initiation of tears may on some occasions be a type of conditioned response. The sights and sounds of a funeral act as stimuli to trigger a tearful reaction, which may be accompanied by an affect of sadness. Some emphasis has been placed on the importance for those who are closely related to the deceased to be able to shed tears at the funeral ceremony, in order to avoid pathological grief reactions. There are

41

differences which depend on personality and gender in the ability to do this. Prescribed mourning rituals may be a source of comfort to the bereaved, as familiar words are spoken, known ceremonies are enacted and the responsibilities of the bereaved are clearly limited and attainable.

Mourning rituals have developed as a result of the needs (physical, emotional, and social) of individuals who have been bereaved, but are modified by the constraints, including social and economic ones, which are imposed, and are coloured by myth and religion.

Mourning practices are closely involved in the initiation of the homeostatic mechanisms of society which enable role transitions to occur, so that, for example, the wife becomes a widow, or the oldest son becomes the new head of the family. The gathering of the family or social network around the grave or in the funeral chapel reinforces the sense of solidarity of the group, indicates the altered nature of the network (minus the living presence of the deceased), and provides emotional support to those most deeply distressed at the time of the ceremony.

KEY VARIABLES IN THE RITUALS OF MOURNING

Important variables in the mourning rituals of a subculture include the degree of rigidity and adherence to traditional practices, the duration, the pace, the social network involved, the professionalisation of key roles, the personalisation of the proceedings, and the acceptable expression of emotions at the funeral ceremony.

A rigid adherence to a tradition from the mother-country may provide a sense of security to a new migrant group and promote group solidarity but presents conflict to the second generation migrant who has adopted some of the mores of the host country. An overrigid adherence to a set of rules may in any case not allow for the spontaneous expression of grief.

The duration of accepted mourning practices may vary from the brief burial ceremony for the early Australian convict or the early American Puritan to a prolonged laying out ritual and funeral ceremony as practised by some religions. The Coptic Church in Egypt holds a funeral service, usually within one day of the death. There is some urgency to bury the body as Egypt is a hot country and the mummification and embalming techniques developed by the Ancient Egyptians have been lost. There are ceremonies subsequently on the third, seventh, fifteenth, and fortieth days following death, with a large photograph of the deceased in front of the congregation. By the fortieth day, the soul or spirit of the dead person is able to leave this world peacefully for the next world. The Muslims in Egypt conduct ceremonies at similar intervals for their deceased. In Southern China a laying out ritual was common in which the corpse was kept for forty-nine days. Initially, for the first few days, the body could be viewed, but was then placed in a coffin. A vigil by the relatives was kept over the body during this period. A ceremonial feast was held by the deceased family every seven days. After the first seven days the soul of the deceased crossed a bridge over a river to the equivalent of purgatory. In the situation following a murder or suicide, an unhappy soul might remain around the place where it lived for some time.

Some European Roman Catholics conduct a memorial service one year after the death in addition to celebrating the annual All Souls Day celebration for departed souls. The Mexican Day of the Dead combines elements of the Roman Catholic All Souls Day with a fiesta, in which bread in the shape of human bones is eaten, sugar candy skulls flaunt death, revelling and excesses occur, but dressing the graves of the deceased, meditative communion with the dead, and mourning all occur as well. This is, in effect, an eternal mourning ritual which is both formalised but relaxed, so that the barrier between the living and the dead may be broken.

The LoDagaa of Northern Ghana conduct funeral ceremonies that last at least six months and are divided into four stages. The first stage lasts for six or seven days and centres around the burial of the corpse and the redistribution of the dead man's roles and property. The second stage culminates in a second ceremony after three weeks at which the cause of death is established. The third stage at the beginning of the rainy season marks the elevation of the deceased to an ancestral status, while the fourth stage following the harvest involves the construction of an ancestral shrine. Goody (1962) has described these customs. It appears that some of these customs separate the dead person from the living, while other customs help to aggregate both the dead person with his ancestors and the bereaved with the living.

Gorer (1965) referred to "time limited mourning" to designate a phased pattern of behavior, with a period of intense grief followed by a return to physical homeostasis and a fuller social life, which takes place in one or more stages. This may occur as part of traditional ritual or in the bereaved who are not following any particular ritual but describe their own behavior in this phased fashion. Twenty-five out of eighty British mourners reported a distinctly phased pattern, which often appeared to be connected with the active practice of prayer and church-going or especially connected with the practices of the Orthodox Jews. Complex mourning rituals practised by the Orthodox Jews which particularly involve the relatives of the deceased occupy the first seven days and focus the attention on the deceased in a concerted way. For eleven months after this the sons or other mourners attend the synagogue twice daily to recite a special prayer for the dead, after which a gravestone is erected and the period of mourning is over. The Orthodox Jews interviewed reported that they found this concentrated mourning therapeutic and their grief was made easier in that they could not hide it.

Traditionally-oriented widows from Southern Europe (and from many other cultures) adopt a lifetime of mourning, wear characteristic black clothes for the rest of their life and do not marry again.

Although the duration and timing of funeral ceremonies in different cultures appears to be diverse, there may be some features in common. The most intensive ceremonies in which grief is more actively expressed appear to take place around the first few days following death. The ceremonies subsequently over the next six or seven weeks may involve an active vigil, in which prayers or intercessions on the behalf of the deceased are made, and the active shifting of social roles is beginning to settle, while the anniversary ceremonies which occur in some cultures act as a reminder of the deceased to the survivors and may further consolidate social roles. Active pangs of grief may be stimulated in close relatives at these anniversary ceremonies, which decrease in intensity as the years pass. Gorer (1965) regarded the period of most intense grief as being between six and twelve weeks which was reflected in the mourning practices in his sample.

The pace of the funeral ceremony effects the emotional atmosphere. A ponderous, slow-moving ceremony may seem appropriate to increase the air of solemnity, but becomes unbearable if taken to an extreme. A period of relief or relaxation from the mourning solemnity may be welcomed by those involved, who are then able to attend to the duties of the funeral and to resume the work of mourning with renewed strength. The pace of a funeral ceremony may be perceived as hurried to close relatives. I observed a woman with a pathological grief reaction who complained that she was distressed during her husband's burial, when the coffin had to be lowered rapidly into the ground, because torrential rain had destabilised the sides of the grave. She felt that there was inadequate time to bid farewell to her husband and that there was a sense of unreality because the final ceremony had been enacted too quickly. The slow pace of funeral processions was criticised by The Funeral Reform Association in Sydney in 1890, who recommended an increase in the pace of the hearse to a quicker than walking pace.

The social network at the funeral may be extensive or restrictive. The surviving numbers of the immediate family are usually involved. In addition, others attending the funeral would reflect the extended family, friends, or working colleagues. The funeral of a prominent public figure may attract a wider network including the general public. The immediate family may feel inhibited by the presence of a large number of strangers and it may be more satisfactory for the funeral ceremony to be smaller and more personal. Modern societies which are urbanised and anonymous with greater geographical "scatter" of surviving family members may lead to fewer family members present at a funeral. A trend towards increased longevity of the population may result in smaller funeral gatherings as there are fewer peers or close family members who are able to attend.

Professionals involved in the rituals which are set in train by death include those who are involved in the medical aspects such as the physician who may certify death or the pathologist who may perform an autopsy, and those professionals who are largely involved in conducting the mourning ceremonies such as the funeral director and priest and those who are involved in working with the corpse, embalming it, dressing it, transporting it or disposing of the remains.

I drew attention to some cultures in which a "joking partner" officiates at the funeral and may be expected to make ceremonial jibes at the deceased (Haig, 1988). This is a formal role assigned to an individual who belongs to a clan different from that of the deceased. Nineteenth century funerals in England sometimes involved professional mourners, including many pall bearers, feathermen, and wailers, the latter group who initiated crying, but some of these roles disappeared with the advent of the twentieth century. At a time of bereavement, when the family may be in a state of shock, its members may have difficulty in taking all the necessary steps or negotiating the organisation of a funeral, and the support and advice of professionals who are knowledgeable and empathic is useful.

The "personalisation" of the proceedings and active participation by relatives or close friends may assist the bereaved, if the funeral is not to be merely an anonymous ritual. A choice in the funeral and post-funeral arrangements may help relatives to feel involved and not altogether helpless. If these arrangements are in accordance with the wishes of the deceased, that would help to increase the individuality of the funeral. A relative reading a piece of scripture at the funeral ceremony or the participation in a communal chant, prayer, or hymn may increase a feeling of involvement. A family priest or friend giving a eulogy may help to promote a feeling of the individuality of the event. Following a funeral in a village in Ireland, the villagers and relatives all made a point of touching the coffin as it proceeded to the graveyard, as a final gesture of farewell.

The accepted expression of emotion at funerals is an important variable which may modify the course of grief in the individual and deserves further consideration.

THE EXPRESSION OF GRIEF AT FUNERALS

There is a wide variation in the outward expression of grief between individuals. Cultural expectations and practices modify this considerably. While traditional Anglo-Saxon Protestant and some Roman Catholic funerals may appear to be restrained occasions without overt or formalised displays of crying, it is increasingly acceptable for individuals to weep openly. The males are often expected to console female relatives who are more visibly displaying grief. However, an attempt to impose traditions regarding the expression of grief on another cultural group may not be well received or may even be deleterious to the grieving process.

The early Puritan settlers in North America discouraged displays of excessive grief, amongst both themselves and the surrounding Indian tribes. The austere Pilgrim attitude to life in which the world was merely a wilderness to be suffered as preparation for a truly significant eternal home resulted in the simple, unembroidered burial in which grief and the expression of emotion were given a low priority. This influence was still evident in the attitude of Benjamin Rush towards grief who wrote in 1835:

> Persons afflicted with grief should be carried from the room in which their relatives have died, nor should they ever see their bodies afterwards. They should by no means be permitted to follow them to the grave.

The suppression of grief was clearly regarded as important by Rush, who advocated the use of opium (a widespread medication at the time) to attain that purpose. It would have been of interest to know whether Julia, his wife, was carried from the room or was prescribed opium after the death of Benjamin. She appeared to manage her grief subsequently by keeping a diary of her thoughts and gradually taking comfort from the possibility of a reunion with Benjamin in a subsequent life.

The mourning of the Yolngu, an Australian Aboriginal people, is dramatic by comparison with the formal expression of grief by the Puritans or the contemporary Anglo-Saxons. Reid (1978) described the practices in which the widow throws herself on the body of her dead husband, screaming and crying uncontrollably. Other women keen loudly, throwing themselves on the ground and striking their heads with sharp objects, such as stones, knives, and the sharp lids of cans. The men are expected to restrain the women, pulling the weapons from their hands. The men who are closely related may cry and occasionally keen, but on the whole the most dramatic grieving is enacted by the women. It was suggested that an individual who was denied the opportunity to take part in formal mourning ceremonies developed a pathological grief reaction.

Fernandez-Marina (1961) described dramatic public displays of grief in Puerto Rican society manifested by seizure-like attacks and uncontrollable emotions ("el ataque") which could be a useful way for the bereaved to express anger.

Mandelbaum (1959) compared the expression of emotion in two American Indian tribes of the Southwest, the Hopi and the Cocapa. The Hopi discourage overt displays of emotion and parents advise their children to weep, if they must, outside the village where they cannot be observed. The women do cry a little and speak of the loss, but there is no formal wailing. The Cocapa, however, become transported into an ecstasy of violent grief behavior with crying, wailing and screaming for twenty-four hours or more until the body is cremated.

Javanese funeral practices blend Muslim and local elements. Mourners are supposed to be calm and undemonstrative and the ritual is supposed to carry the mourner through grief without severe emotional disturbance. Mandelbaum (1959) discussed how these practices, which depended on a close-knit social group, were less effective when transplanted to a less integrated urban area.

Expressions of happiness may be admixed with grief in societies in which there is a strong belief in an idealised afterlife. The Maoris, whilst expressing grief, regard a funeral as a happy occasion, as the deceased is going to join his ancestors. Some Christian churches express grief and joy at the funeral service if the deceased is thought to have a passport to heaven.

Sexual differences in the expression of grief were demonstrated by Frankel et al. (1982) in the Huli people of Papua New Guinea. Females are expected to express their emotions openly at a "duguanda" (crying house) where the body is laid out on a platform. The women weep freely, rocking and chutching at the body. The keening is stylised and climaxes at the internment on the following day. The men take no part in these activities, but construct the coffin and dig the grave. As the coffin is lowered into the ground, one or two men may weep briefly and then silently. The author suggested that the marked contrast between the mourning practices of the men and women could have been associated with excess mortality in the Huli widowers in the first year of bereavement, Huli widows showing no such tendency.

It seems that in many cultures men are more restrained than women in the outward expression of grief at funeral ceremonies. These gender differences in the expression of grief may relate to intrinsic biological differences in addition to cultural influences in the expression of a range of emotions (see Haig, 1988).

A funeral ceremony which is socially sanctioned and congruent with the belief system of the individuals is important for the process of normal mourning. The bereaved individual usually values the opportunity to participate in a ceremony in which grief is both expressed and acknowledged. The expression of grief may include crying, facial and bodily expressions of sadness and verbal communications whose content is primarily culturally determined. The postures and verbalisations of grief may be reflected in mourning ceremonies which have adapted to incorporate the profound affects which are expressed, in addition to reflecting the society in which they take place.

The ritualisation of grief in the mourning ceremonies provides an element of control and may help in setting boundaries for the individual and provide a guide as to what is permissible in a particular society. In addition, some mourning ceremonies provide an example of how the individual could grieve. For individuals who are "frozen" in their grief, the rituals of mourning may provide a stimulus which triggers normal grief. In addition, the observation of a group of relatives or peers who are grieving may reassure the individual of his normality in feeling grief-stricken, may provide him an example of how to grieve and also provide him with reassuring identifications with those around.

Viewing the body of the deceased may be of importance in order to bring home the reality of the death (in addition to ensuring that "foul play" has not occurred). Some ceremonies include "viewing" the body and "paying the last respects" to the corpse. Initial feelings of numbness or disbelief after viewing the body would often be followed by open expressions of grief. The initial feelings of disbelief may be accompanied by uncertainty as to the true identity of the corpse, as, even if expertly prepared, it may look different to the appearance of the individual in life. If the bereaved person is aware of the details of the embalming process, the sense of unreality may be heightened, as the internal organs of the deceased have been removed and replaced with padding. There has been some debate about the importance of viewing the body and touching or holding it following neonatal death (see Chapter 11) but this area has not been systematically explored following the death of adults.

Some mourning practices may also give recognition to the depth of involvement of the most closely bereaved, by relieving them of their everyday responsibilities, or even feeding them, in the rituals of Orthodox Jewry.

Guilt in the bereaved may be assuaged by involvement in a ritual, with its associated effort and expense, which helps to atone for the aggressive feelings which may have been harbored towards the deceased.

It is concluded that while mourning ceremonies have the potential to assist in initiating and promoting the course of grief, there is a wide range of responses as to their perceived usefulness by the bereaved individual. Some individuals require more time than is available in the typical Western-style funeral ceremony to begin to absorb the implications of the death and contemplate on it. Too many abstractions and symbolic representations in a funeral ceremony may not resonate with the needs of the bereaved who require the presentation of simple realities. For the increasing number of individuals who are not affiliated with any religious group, the development of secular funeral ceremonies and subsequent mourning rituals which are acceptable and promote the expression of normal grief are required.

THE NEMESIS OF FUNERAL PRACTICES
IN MIGRANT SETTLEMENTS

Funeral practices follow the vagaries of fashion. They are shaped by economic realities as well as being influenced by changing attitudes in migrants and settlers who later become the conservative culture carriers.

In the first part of the nineteenth century the austere Pilgrim attitude to funerals was gradually replaced in North America by a more personal attitude towards the deceased, with the result that the dead were becoming more treasured and the body more respected, with more elaborate coffins (named "caskets", which implied that they contained treasure), more complex funeral ceremonies, and pleasantly landscaped rural cemeteries. An interest in spiritualism and communion with the dead was in evidence both in America and Britain. Jackson (1980) outlined the continuing developments in the United States with a diminution in the direct involvement with the dying and a decrease in ritual and formal mourning practices in the latter part of the twentieth century. He characterised the current situation in America as a dichotomisation of the worlds of the living and dead which has resulted from the forces of urbanisation, mobility and demographic changes. He considered that there had been a withdrawal from commitment to the dead. The funerals of the elderly may require less acknowledgement of the passing, as they would usually be "low-grief" situations for the survivors. Kinship ties may also be weaker in contemporary America. Less emphasis on a belief in the after-life and a diminution of religious belief in general may have also contributed to a decline in the importance of the funeral. Death itself and the decay of the body may be regarded as a subject too horrible to contemplate as has been suggested by Gorer (1965), who refers to a "pornography of death." While it has been suggested that the culture of individualism, the weakening of traditional social ties, and the demise of ritual may place the bereaved under greater strain with the possibility of an increase in pathological grief reactions, which was partially suggested by Gorer (1965), it was pointed out by Osterweis et al. (1984) that no research had at that time demonstrated an increase in negative health consequences in the Western world.

In contrast to the early Puritan settlers in North America, the early Australian white settlers were convicts and soldiers, who, while lacking the religious leanings of their American brothers, would have shared a disdain for ritual, would have maintained a simple cameraderie, and would have conducted brief and simple funerals.

Griffin (1982) outlined the historical aspects of Australian funeral practices. Within a few years of arrival in Sydney in 1790 many of the "Second Fleet," which consisted of convicts and their guardians, had died, necessitating the opening of many burial grounds in and around Sydney, many of which have been obliterated. Funerals were conducted according to the rites of the Anglican Church, although as many as a third of the convicts were Roman Catholics and some were nonconformist Protestants and Jews. The Anglican monopoly created much ill-will, and by 1820 Roman Catholic chaplains were appointed and sectarian areas of cemeteries were being established.

Early Australian graves were often simple mounds of earth with a wooden grave-marker which was cheap, readily available and easy to work. As the settlements developed, so did the burial grounds, although not everyone chose to use them. David Collins (who was a governor of New South Wales) described a man who buried his wife and child near to his own front door and who was later seen pouring rum on the grave since his wife was so fond of it during her life. Samuel Marsden, an early chaplain who was about to perform the funeral rites over an ex-convict who had been stabbed was preempted by the man's mates who had already buried him "in the most beastly manner, after pronouncing the most horrid oaths, curses, and imprecations over his corpse." Lone burials away from established burial grounds were often performed if there was a fear of infectious disease, such as smallpox. During the rush to the gold fields of Victoria and New South Wales, deaths from accident and infectious disease were not uncommon, and bush burials were sometimes primitive. In the cities such as Melbourne, Sydney, Adelaide, or Hobart, where wealth was accumulating, larger and more elaborate funerals were taking place in the nineteenth century. The outback burial required handyman skills. Arch Burnett described the burial of his grandfather at Tinga Tingana cattle station in 1917:

> "We buried him beneath a Queensland bean tree on the bank of the Strzelecki. . . . My mate and I made a headstone from cement and cut letters out of sheet lead with a pocket knife. We set them in the cement, placed the stone on his grave and surrounded it with iron railings which we made in the station blacksmith shop."

The more elaborate and complex rituals of the nineteenth century funeral in the Australian cities were also described by Griffin (1982).

One rule book of 1885 distinguished four different degrees of mourning dress, which reflected the relationship to the deceased and the length of time that had elapsed since the death. A better class of funeral procession included "female mourners," young women dressed in white, "mutes," who were professional mourners, who were male, remained mute and carried a stave draped with a black or white silk cloth, described for the first time in 1811, pall bearers, pages and feathermen, who were all derived from earlier English traditions. Sometimes the pall was draped over the bearers as well as the coffin leading to the comment by Charles Dickens that the whole looked like a blind monster with twelve human legs. A featherman headed the procession. He carried a tray full of large feathers on his head, consisting of black ostrich plumes (or white ones if the deceased was young or unmarried). This latter custom probably had its origins in medieval heraldry associated with the funeral of a baron, who possessed a helmet with a plume of feathers.

A reaction against the increasingly elaborate nature of funerals in Australia developed. In 1875 the Funeral Reform Association was founded and in 1890 recommended a number of simplifications to funerals, including a plain coffin, plain hearse, no pall over the coffin, no mutes, no pall bearers, no funeral procession, no invitation to a funeral in public print, the abandonment of elaborate mourning clothes, and the speeding up of the funeral procession. Gradually, with the movement for cremation on sanitary and practical grounds gaining acceptance in the cities, funerals became less elaborate. With the massacre of many young men from Australia and Britain in the First World War, a succession of elaborate and expensive funeral ceremonies became demoralising and less meaningful, and consequently funeral practices were simplified at that time.

After the Second World War, Australia was opened up to migrants from many different countries, bringing with them their traditions and customs with the result that there is now a wide range of funeral practices deriving from all parts of Asia, Europe, and the Pacific Basin. It will be of interest to observe how they develop and the practices which are adopted by the second generation migrants. There are some causes of friction which develop as a result of different funeral practices by migrant groups. Greek, Italian, and Turkish funerals generally allow for a more unrestrained venting of feelings which may not be recognised practice in the Anglo-Saxon prevailing culture. Muslim funerals and burial practices may be at distinct variance with local Australian laws and customs.

The Muslim practice of public wailing, allowing the body to remain in the home, followed by rapid burial, without a coffin and facing Mecca, are all factors which may create difficulties.

Tracing the overall trends in Australian funeral practices, it is possible to observe a development from the crude burials with an Anglican service imposed, in the early days of the colony, to fairly elaborate funerals in the cities and townships, in the latter part of the nineteenth century, which almost seem like an embellished funeral based on the English practices of fifty years earlier. Funerals became more simplified again around the time of the First World War. With the coming of migrant groups from diverse cultures, the range of funeral practices is expanding.

THE POLITICAL NATURE OF FUNERAL PRACTICES

Every funeral makes some statement to society about the status, family and social network of the individual. A low key funeral may convey the message that a particular death is a private matter. The following epitaph, which was quoted by Griffin et al. (1982), could be taken as a statement about the death of a man which had a zero impact on society:

> "Beneath this stone Sam Bodin lies,
> No one laughs and no one cries.
> Where he's gone, and how he fares,
> No one knows, and no one cares."

The statement may be actively promoted or expanded on by individuals with vested interests. Bereavement is a time of heightened emotional arousal which may be directed into various channels, which sometimes include anger which may take the form of revenge against an identified transgressor or enemy. Examples of this sort include the highly politicised funerals of Northern Ireland, in which murderous resentment against the political opposition is readily fuelled as a result of the increased emotional arousal and suggestibility of a large crowd of mourners.

A death may be disruptive to the social structure and result in a period of disorganisation, which is resolved by the parties involved attempting to reconstruct a functional organisation which is acceptable. Some of the most intensive political activity occurs around the time of a death. This activity is reflected in the funeral arrangements which may themselves act as a catalyst to the political activity.

The funeral of a statesman may represent the end of an era and be dutifully observed by the majority of the population, including the opponents. The highly elaborate nature of some state funerals is a sign of respect for an eminent person or office, but may in addition reflect insecurity about the possibility of social change. Childe (1945) contended that funeral rituals become more elaborate when the existence of a community is under threat.

The funeral of a head of state or leader may serve as an opportunity for the population to identify the heir. In addition, the heir may, on this occasion, undergo some personal realignment and identify more strongly with, or incorporate some of the attributes of his predecessor.

It is remarkable that three Asian women who were not the hereditary heirs to the positions of their deceased male relatives (who were murdered) all became political leaders themselves. These were President Cory Aquino in the Philippines, Sirimavo Bandaranaike, who became Prime Minister in Ceylon, and Benazir Bhutto who was for a time the leader of the Opposition in Pakistan. These women presumably had a strong sense of mission and justice stirred up by the violent deaths of their menfolk. However, the mantle of office could only have been attained by receiving the support of a sizeable section of the community. The public's perception of the dynamics of these deaths and funeral arrangements would have contributed to this support.

The funeral which has provoked the most debate and controversy on a world scale in recent times has been that of the Japanese Emperor, Hirohito, following his death on January 7th 1989. He was the longest ruling monarch on earth (ruling for over sixty years), was descended from a thousand-year dynasty and was regarded as a divine being by many of his subjects. He was nevertheless a mild-mannered man, who was regarded as being somewhat reclusive with an interest in marine biology, but succeeded in persuading his militant generals to accept a peaceful but humiliating surrender at the end of the Pacific War. After this, he functioned as Head of State in a Japan which was rebuilding to its present economic strength.

Following his death, the younger generation in Japan was probably less moved than the older generation, the stock market did not collapse as predicted, and a state funeral was held on February 24th. Prior to the funeral there was some fear that powerful right-wing minority groups who supported the concept of the "Divinity of the Emperor" would use the funeral to gain popular support for this notion and for their own promotion. The Japanese Catholic Archbishop, Kikawada, expressed condolences, but warned against deifying the Emperor. The public funeral ceremony did not refer to the Emperor's divinity, although there was a private Shinto funeral ceremony conducted afterwards.

Outside Japan there was heated debate in countries which had experienced invasion or atrocities at the hands of Japan as to the appropriateness of representation, if any, at the Emperor's funeral. The tendency to eulogise about the Emperor was met with acrimonious debate. *The Guardian Weekly* of January 15th 1989 reported criticisms by representatives from both sides of the British Parliament about message of condolence sent by the Queen and the Prime Minister, Mrs. Thatcher, saying that it would have been an insult to thousands of prisoners of war killed and tortured by the Japanese if Britain were officially represented at the funeral.

Eventually the British were represented at the funeral by the Duke of Edinburgh and the British Foreign Secretary, Sir Geoffrey Howe. The Dutch Royal Family did not attend. *The Washington Post* leader praised Hirohito's decision to surrender in 1945 which saved uncounted Japanese lives and American lives as well and praised him as a man with a surer sense of balance than his advisers. The President Elect, George Bush, attended the funeral.

The funeral itself appeared to take place without incident. The Emperor could be seen as symbolising different facets of Japanese culture. He could be viewed as a supporter of war or a bringer of peace and reconciliation. His divine mantle slipped away in the eyes of many Japanese, although the older generation sometimes clung to this belief. The attitude towards him aroused ambivalent feelings, but it appeared that, in the end, political and economic expediency were the most powerful forces in shaping the decisions of nations as to their representation at that funeral.

THE DIGNIFIED DISPOSAL OF THE BODY AND SOCIOCULTURAL FACTORS

What happens to the body after death depends on an amalgam of social necessity, religious belief, and individual inclination, not necessarily in that order.

The dignified burial or disposal of the body may be a hallmark of the rise of human civilisation. I recently walked on the shore of a dried up inland sea at Lake Mungo in Australia. It is now semiarid desert with vivid ochre colors and weather-sculpted shapes. In the last Ice Age there was a thriving human settlement here. Some of the world's earliest graves have been discovered here, which are around 30,000 years old. One contained the bones of a woman, broken into small pieces, while the other had been carefully covered with red ochre, which suggested some formal burial rituals at that time.

The simple hygienic need to dispose of a body rapidly in a hot climate has undoubtedly influenced the rapidity with which burial is performed in many Middle Eastern countries. A shortage of materials for coffins or the lack of embalming techniques could also modify burial practices. Below ground burial may be precluded by rocky terrain or the situation in Rotorua, New Zealand, in which hot springs are released by digging. Cremation may sometimes be favoured on the grounds of public health.

Religious beliefs and traditions have also played a prominent part in these practices. The Tibetans provide an interesting example of a culture which utilises a variety of methods for disposal of the corpse, including celestial burial, water burial, cremation, burial in the ground, and internment in a stupa, described by Phuntso (1981). Celestial burial, which is used for the majority of the population, takes place three to five days after the initial mourning ceremonies. The corpse is laid on a high rock platform and a fire is lit next to it, the smoke attracting the sacred vultures. The undertaker dissects small pieces of flesh from the corpse which he feeds to the vultures, together with bones crushed with tsampa. If any bone is left it is burned to ashes and scattered. When the body has been entirely disposed of, the soul is then free to leave. Water burial, which consists of throwing the corpse, which may be clad in a white cloth, into a river, is used for beggars, widows, widowers, and the very poor. Individuals who die of contagious diseases and criminals are buried in the ground. Learned scholars and persons of high rank are cremated, releasing their souls. The most important Lamas are embalmed with spices and placed in a religious monument known as a stupa. While these practices are supported by religious beliefs, there may be socioeconomic factors which determine, for example, that the majority of the population are (or used to be) given celestial burial, which is an effective means of disposal of the body in mountainous terrain. It is noteworthy that the religious explanations for what happens, such as "the vultures are holy birds," or "feeding the fishes is a present to Buddha," or "after cremation the soul is free to rise to heaven" are culturally acceptable myths to ease the discomfort of relatives who may still feel an emotional attachment to the body. Even the agnostic in Western societies uses comforting clichés or modern myths to reassure himself after the death of a loved one, such as "she is at peace now" or "he will feel no more pain because he no longer exists." (This latter statement presents a paradox of logic which is probably insoluble!)

De Spelder et al. (1987) discussed different means of disposal of the body which in earlier societies were strongly influenced by religious belief. The Ancient Egyptians believed in a life after death in which there was a bipartite soul, consisting of the "Ba," which remained in the corpse, and the "Ka," which proceeded to the afterlife. Mummification of the body was necessary so that the Ba would have a home. Platform burial was favoured by the Indians of the American plains. If the heaven is regarded as being celestial there is a certain logic in locating the corpse in an elevated position or on a mountain top.

The practices of the Parsis in which the body is placed in the Tower of Silence to be devoured by the vultures avoids the defilement of the sacred elements of earth, fire, or water by death. However, the neighbouring Hindu community disposes of the body by cremation on a funeral pyre as it is believed that the embodied self casts off worn-out bodies and enters into others that are new.

Seafarers who were on long voyages had, by necessity, to dispose of a corpse using sea burial with the appropriate ceremony. However, the modern cruise liner, with its quota of senior citizens has its own refrigerated morgue facilities.

It is of interest to note that most ceremonies of disposal of the body are performed in a dignified manner by an individual who has a special role. To dispose of the bodies of one's own dead relative would be a painful task.

If it is not possible to dispose of the body according to custom, utilising the appropriate professional helper, major discomfort may be experienced by the relatives and this interferes with the grieving processes.

CONCLUSIONS

Mourning rituals, which vary considerably both cross-culturally and intraculturally, serve as a framework within which grief may be expressed in addition to shaping the expression of that grief. Mourning rituals are of importance for the deceased, who is after all at the centre of the ceremony. However the rituals are probably of more importance to the bereaved and to the society in which the funeral takes place. Both the bereaved individual and the surrounding social network may need to grieve and to achieve a homeostasis of relationships which may be expedited by the rituals of mourning.

Mourning rituals which are congruent with a particular individual's culture, promote grieving, provide comforting social support, and are in tune with that individual's "biological grief clock" are, in general, beneficial.

The expression of grief which is acceptable at funerals shows interesting cross-cultural differences. The options of uninhibited catharsis, a stiff upper lip and suppression, or the employment of professional wailers to "call the tune" may not mesh with the needs of the individual. Most bereaved people do require an opportunity to express grief, but in their own time, at their own pace, and in their own communicative style. The funeral ceremony itself may not always be the ideal venue for this.

Funerals in the political arena can be a focal microcosm, in addition to being catalysts and movers of public opinion. Powerful emotions are generated by a funeral which may be harnessed or manipulated and give rise to political change or reaction.

The dignified disposal of the body depends on an admixture of pragmatic factors, which include environmental and technological considerations, and cultural beliefs and attitudes.

Funeral practices evolve over a relatively short period in societies in response to cultural, social, and economic forces, as exemplified by the progress of American and Australian funerals from simple to complex ceremonies, which will perhaps, with "Green" environmentalist influences, return to a simple but nonsectarian ceremony in the future.

Chapter 8

SYMBOLS AND THE DECEASED

Mankind wittingly or unwittingly leaves memorials to his existence, which remain, sometimes for centuries. The memorials of the twentieth century, which could conceivably still be apparent several centuries hence, include concrete freeways and skyscrapers (in spite of the cancer that we are now informed affects concrete), dust-bowls where once there were forests, and garbage tips which contain everything from rusting automobiles to "disposable" (but nondestructible) diapers and syringes. Hopefully, the above items will not be the only legacy we leave to the future.

On an individual and societal level, monuments are erected and memorials created which are dedicated to the dead. In addition chronological markers develop which focus on the deceased.

MEMORIALS

The memorials which survive after the funeral service is over include the material ones which are readily observable by the public, such as tombstones, sometimes with an epitaph, plaques, gardens, the barrows of the neolithic chieftains, the pyramids of the Pharaohs, the tombs of the Ming Emperors, the mausoleums of the communist leaders or a simple wooden marker over a grave. The Maori meeting houses in New Zealand serve as a type of memorial and link the present generation to the ancestors in a very close way. The meeting house is named after an important ancestor and the structure of the buildings is symbolically likened to parts of his or her body, with the ridge pole likened to the backbone, the rafters to the ribs and the barge boards to the outstretched limbs. Thus, for the Maoris, assembling in the meeting house enabled them to draw strength, support and knowledge from the ancestors around them. The large public memorial may serve to emphasise the importance of the status of an individual or may have a political or religious purpose, to reinforce a belief system in the population. A public

59

memorial, such as a war memorial, may serve as a focus for communal grief, national pride, or a warning to the population of the futility of war.

Other memorials which are less visible but of great value to the bereaved include personal mementos such as a photograph of the deceased, a letter, a lock of hair, or an article of clothing. A personal memorial such as a donation to a charity or the establishment of a trust may reflect the interests of that person or the way in which death occurred.

A domestic memorial which occurs in some cultures is the family altar. In Japan it is customary for a widow to cultivate a dialogue with the deceased husband at the family altar. This was examined by Yamamoto et al. (1969) who found that the widows derived some comfort from this practice.

The body itself may be visibly incorporated in the memorial so that an embalmed corpse or relics, which consist of bones or fragments of the bodies of deceased religious personages, become the focus of attention. The practice of keeping bones on display in a charnel house (which was also a centre of social activity and meeting) was current in the Middle Ages in Europe and emphasised the accepted familiarity with death in those times (see De Spelder et al., 1987).

The funerary objects which have been buried with the deceased reflect the religious beliefs and personal idiosyncracies of the time and often become closely identified with the memorial. These have ranged from the simple utensils of the day, which may be required in the next life, to the life-size pottery army of the Ching Emperor in Xian, which was intended to protect him at the time of his reincarnation.

Burial with a favorite trinket or in the best clothes may reassure the bereaved that they are doing everything possible for the deceased. The thought that one will be buried in a family vault close to other members of the family may be comforting.

FUNCTIONS OF MEMORIALS

Memorials may serve principally to remind the family and the world of the life and death of an individual. As well as serving as a stimulus to memories, they may also serve as a warning.

They may serve other functions. A heavy gravestone may prevent a body from rising from the grave prematurely (a belief which was current in several cultures, including Finland). If the spirit of the deceased is looking on, he may be reassured by observing that he has a properly tended grave.

However, one process which may occur in the bereaved is that the memorial (or a memento) itself comes to represent the deceased person in a compelling fashion. The grave, mausoleum or memorial becomes invested by the bereaved person with some attributes of the dead person. This may be very convenient, as the bereaved person can then control the deceased and can avoid, visit, or relocate the deceased. Alternatively, this process may be somewhat eerie and the bereaved may feel haunted. Aboriginal Australians acknowledge this in their culture which is an animistic one, in which rocks, trees, and landscape features become invested with some of the spirits and characteristics of the ancestors. This projection of some of the perceived attributes of the dead person into a memorial (which takes place without the bereaved person being fully aware of what is occurring) may result in the bereaved feeling muddled, weak, or in some sense threatened, particularly if the relationship in life was an ambivalent one. This "cult of the memorial" or a persistent relationship with the grave of the beloved is not uncommon regardless of whether the individual has strongly based religious beliefs or not. For some branches of the Christian Church, emphasis is placed on taking bread and wine in the Communion ceremony, which is a memorial to Christ, the bread representing his body and the wine representing his blood. Jackson (1959) suggested that a ritual like the Mass could serve a useful purpose in working through feelings of guilt, incorporation or substitution in the bereaved.

A very personal memorial for an individual often exists which is known only to intimate relatives or friends, such as a chair in which the deceased used to sit, or a place which he used to visit. This may act as a stimulus to memories about the deceased and may be more satisfactory than a memorial in stone, bronze, or concrete.

CHRONOLOGICAL MARKERS

Regular visits to the grave of the deceased, anniversary ceremonies, anniversary newspaper notices, the keeping of diaries, or the occurrence of religious or family festivals all serve to act as reminders of the deceased.

An obligation to the dead which is fulfilled through an anniversary or other ritual may, in addition to providing a sense of having performed one's duty, also give an opportunity for a reevaluation of the relationship, both past and present, with the deceased. The chronological markers also have an effect of reminding the individual of his own mortality and demise.

Regular visits to a grave may be impractical in a society in which there is urbanised scatter, or geographical dislocation of migrants, and it appears that there is now less emphasis on this type of activity, which may have a long-term effect on grieving. It may be of importance in a society in flux to have other ways of marking anniversaries of bereavement in a meaningful way.

THE CONTROL OF GRIEF:
RITUAL AND THE AGE OF REASON

Mourning rituals may be a means of modulating excesses of grief, by bringing a process which is potentially disruptive for the individual or for society into the ambit of a set of socially sanctioned rituals, with increased possibility for control. Other, more direct attempts to control grief have been attempted by injunctions, advice and consolations to the bereaved, and by attempts by the bereaved themselves to alter the pattern.

Attempts to control grief in Anglo Saxon culture have been described in sixteenth century English literature by Pigman (1985). In the early sixteenth century there was a tendency to be very concerned about grief which was regarded as subversive of the rule of reason and disruptive to domestic and social order. The expression of grief was thought to reveal irrationality, weakness, and inadequate self control. Certain theologians condemned all mourning as evidence of a lack of faith, while others counselled moderation in mourning. The purpose of "consolation" at that time was to induce the bereaved to suppress grief. By the seventeenth century more tolerant attitudes appeared to be emerging. Shakespeare, writing in the late sixteenth century, does not hesitate to describe grief and suggest that the verbalisation of grief may be therapeutic.

What! Man: ne'er pull your hat upon your brows:
Give sorrow words: the grief that does not speak
Whispers the o'er fraught heart and bids it break.
Macduff in Macbeth iv, iii, 208.

The early American Puritans deemphasised the funeral ceremony and the expression of grief, as this life was merely a preparation for the next (Jackson, 1980). There was a disapproving attitude towards excesses of grief (which could be seen as being critical of the will of God) still current in the early nineteenth century. This was described by Thielman et al. (1986) in his examination of Julia Rush's Diary. Julia Rush, the wife of Benjamin Rush, (the physician with a major interest in psychiatry) documented her thoughts about the loss of her husband over a period of thirty-three years in her diary. As a pietistic Protestant, she used ritualised religious language (peppered with Biblical quotes) to express her feelings and redefine painful thoughts. She also made entries on the anniversary of Benjamin's death annually for five years following his death. One final death anniversary was noted eight years after his death when painful memories of Benjamin appeared to be fading. She increasingly made entries on her birthday, focusing on her own life, its shortcomings, and her own sense of salvation despite her deficiencies. The strategies she used appeared to resemble a "cognitive reframing" technique, in that she transformed her initial assessment of the situation, which emphasised Benjamin's death as God's chastisement of her for her worldliness, into an assessment in which she accepted the inevitability of her own death and saw in death the eventual possibility of union with God and a reunion with her loved ones. Thus she was able, using her framework of Christian beliefs of that time to attribute future meaning and comfort to a painful situation of past loss.

Rosenblatt (1983) discussed the use of self-control and attempts to minimise grief and avoid reminders demonstrated in the writings of other nineteenth century diarists. The attitudes of the diarists, in which there were attempts not to offend God by either being overcritical of him or setting up the deceased as an object of reverence could have led to an attempt to suppress feelings of grief, or rationalise them in a similar manner to Julia Rush in her diary.

In an increasingly individualistic (and heterogeneous) society such as the United States or Australia, it is often regarded as the right of the individual to express feelings in the way he or she chooses without undue interference from those around. However, in practice, the individual is constrained by the social milieu. There may be embarrassment to conservative Australians when an ethnic funeral is accompanied by overt expressions of grief, or by stylised wailing. Consolations following a typical Australian funeral may still consist of injunctions to the bereaved such as "stop crying and pull yourself together" or "It's not the end of the world" or "You'll find another wife," which tend to arouse irritation in the bereaved, who experience a major empathic dysjunction, and also experience doubts over the legitimacy of experienced grief.

While modern evidence suggests that grief requires some avenues of expression, otherwise pathological outcomes may result, it is not clear whether "catharsis" or an unmodulated expression of grief which is not accompanied by some changes in attitude towards the self or world is helpful. If this catharsis is not accompanied by a perception of understanding social support, then it is unlikely that the catharsis will be beneficial.

THE CONTROL OF GRIEF THROUGH LANGUAGE

The experience of grief may be so painful that it has to be "dosed" so that the pain is not paramount for too long. The "dosing" may be an automatic mechanism, and result in waves of grief alternating with periods of numbness. Deliberate techniques of controlling grief may also be employed, such as distraction with other activities, or avoidance of reminders, such as concealing the photograph of the deceased, but the most commonly utilised techniques are linguistic in nature and involve suppression or limitation of expression of grief using self-commands and rationalisation in which the deceased is now viewed as "at peace" or hope for a future reunion is contemplated.

The deceased and his attributes may be symbolised and encoded in language. Words (which are symbols anyway) can be stored, retrieved, manipulated, rearranged, and sometimes lost or merely mislaid. The use of this language is a facility which is to some extent under the control of the bereaved. Memories of the deceased can be reactivated by key words, and the deceased may himself be represented by words which have an affective significance, and can be modified over time. The ability to use language which is dependent on education and the brain substrate may thus influence the course of grief and sometimes expedite it.

Rosenblatt (1983) has raised the possibility that individuals with fewer words (such as children and the mentally retarded) experience less grief because they are less likely to trigger off grief with their limited vocabulary. I would suggest that their grief is likely to be as intense in those individuals, although expressed differently, and over a different time frame. The ability to control grief through the use of language may be increased in individuals who can use appropriate verbal symbols to represent their feelings.

CHAPTER 9

DEVELOPMENT AND GRIEF

Do ye hear the children weeping, O my brothers,
Ere the sorrow comes with years?

The Cry of the Children
Elizabeth Barrett Browning

Bereavement, at different stages of the life cycle, results in specific reactions, which on the surface appear diverse. The fretful or colicky baby, the resentful toddler, the sad school girl, the acting out adolescent boy, the bereft young mother, the agitated and grief-stricken widow, or the guilt ridden but inebriated widower, may all be manifesting grief following a bereavement. Whilst the mourning process described by psychoanalysts may only fully develop in adolescence, most individuals throughout the life cycle react to the loss of a close relationship with distress of some sort, which is known as grief. Affective, cognitive, and motor components of grief differ with the developmental stage, personality and individual circumstances of the bereavement.

TYPES OF LOSS

A distinction between different types of loss, such as a partial loss, resulting from temporary separation, or a permanent loss, resulting from bereavement is important. For the infant, there may be little distinction between the two, a separation lasting for more than a short time being perceived in an identical way to a permanent loss and resulting in a similar adverse reaction, but for the school-aged child an untimely separation from a parent may be perceived in a different way to the loss of that parent through death. An adolescent may regard a planned separation with excitement, or as a badge of independence, whereas an ageing adult may regard a separation with pessimism and a grief reaction, as the likelihood of reunion (in this life) is small.

An expected loss, may often be less traumatic than an unexpected loss, provided there has been the opportunity for anticipatory "working through" of the loss and planning alternative coping strategies. An example of an expected loss is that of a woman whose recently retired spouse has experienced increasing ill-health and a series of heart attacks, culminating in a very restricted life style. She has had several years to consider the possibility of her husband's demise and has even gone through a period of anticipatory grieving following his most recent massive heart attack. An example of an unexpected loss is that of a young mother who comes home to find that her husband has been killed in a road accident and is immediately confronted with a major emotional adjustment in addition to having to cope with major economic and social changes in her life which were unforeseen.

A "timely death" is less traumatic than an "untimely death," so that the death of an elderly parent who has lived a good "three score years and ten" is of less emotional and functional concern than the loss of a young spouse or the loss of mother in childhood. The loss may be of a relationship with the "primary object" which usually involves the mother, in childhood, or with a "secondary object," which may involve another person, a pet, or a toy. Loss of a primary object early in childhood, which is an untimely loss, would, at first sight, appear to result in a grief reaction which has little resemblance to that of the adult. The young child may respond with apparent indifference, anger, or a temporary regression and may switch its emotional allegiances to another caretaker with some rapidity, and only grieve fully with yearning and memories of the lost parent some years later. The primary object at this early stage is essential for both physical and emotional survival and a hiatus in the primary bond is avoided, with the infant or young child attempting to find a substitute source of emotional and physical protection as soon as possible. The loss of an elderly mother with a terminal cancer by an adult who has successfully established his own mature relationships is an example of a "timely" loss which usually results in grief, with regret, sorrow, yearning, and some comforting memories of her in her healthier days, but with an admixture of relief that she is now no longer in pain and is at rest. The urgent need for mother for physical survival and emotional development would have long since receded in such a situation. An ability to conceptualise and review her death in the perspective of a fulfilled life and an ability to obtain emotional gratification from a variety of other sources, would also soften the blow.

The type of loss may be categorised by relationship to the deceased.

Most studies have focused on loss of spouse in adult life with an increasing interest in the immediate and longer-term effects of maternal loss in childhood, although, with the increase in child custody cases with fathers contesting the "divine right" of women to be the custodian, there has been an increased interest in the effects of paternal loss in childhood. Countries at war, in which there is a differential loss of young males compared to females, contend with the problem of paternal loss in childhood and this has been examined by Kaffman, Elizur, and Gluckson (1987) in Israel. Sibling loss and loss of children at different ages provoke differing reactions, while the effects of abortion, miscarriage, and stillbirth may provoke psychological reactions, which are becoming increasingly socially sanctioned. Attention has been focussed on the loss of homosexual partners. Clearly a full gamut of grief reactions may occur, and in a study by Martin (1988) it appeared that homosexual men were experiencing considerable distress in coping with AIDS-related bereavements.

The loss of a secondary object, such as a pet, may cause grief, but if that pet has become a major focus of life or has come to symbolise others, such as children, then grief would be correspondingly more severe. If the relationship with the pet is nonconflicted, it may be possible to express grief over its loss more readily than in an ambivalent relationship with a human being, hence the appearance of a full blown grief reaction in a woman whose pet dog died, although showing primarily bitterness and resentment when her spouse died.

Clearly in this latter situation the intensity of the attachment altered the grief reaction. This intensity of attachment may be assessed on the basis of the time and quality of interaction and fantasies (day dreaming and dreaming) about the object.

DIVERSE VARIABLES AND GRIEF

Attitudes of an individual towards death and dying modify the grief reaction and its outward expression. These attitudes are formed throughout life and are dependent on the stage of cognitive development, the information available to the individual and his cultural background. The grief reaction is also influenced by the psychological conflicts which involve the deceased (or departed), personality factors, which may be genetically determined and involve basic neurophysiological response profiles, family dynamics, intrafamilial and extrafamilial support and concurrent stressors, both physical and psychological. A bereaved child may not be able to verbalise or work through a loss unless there is a secure attachment to an adult (Sekaer, 1987).

Some of the manifestations of grief may result from an alteration in physiological functioning. Basic biological ties to another individual may be mediated through the senses of sight, smell, sound, and touch, and act as "zeitgebers," as proposed by Hofer (1984), which may influence the chronobiological mechanisms, or put more simply may "set the biological clock." When these zeitgebers are interrupted, as happens in a bereavement, the chronobiological mechanisms are disrupted, resulting in some of the characteristics of a grief reaction, such as sleep disturbance, loss of appetite, disorientation, and irritability.

An examination of reaction to loss (particularly through bereavement) and attitudes to death throughout the life cycle follows. Attention is drawn to the cognitive developmental stages described by Piaget (1973), which help to clarify attitudes towards and understanding of death in different age groups.

THE INFANT—THE SENSORIMOTOR STAGE

The reaction of an infant bereaved of its mother depends on biological, psychological, and social factors. In the preverbal infant it is easier to delineate the biological and social factors rather than the psychological factors. For a young baby in a hostile environment, the loss of mother could be catastrophic, resulting in physical risks ranging from starvation to those such as infections and objective household dangers of which the infant would be totally unaware. A six-week infant, who had previously had a relaxed interaction with mother, and was accustomed to her breast, her handling, her routine, her smell, and her noises, would be devastated by her disappearance, to be replaced by a series of different caretakers, of varying responsiveness, with calloused hands, bony ribs, sharp voices, and proffering a bottle with an evil smelling rubber teat, with an indigestible concoction inside. The initial reaction to such a major environmental change would probably be one of distress in most infants. It could be hypothesised that the major component of distress resulted from physical discomfort, dietary changes, and changes in the environmental stimuli to which the infant had become accustomed and by which the "biological clock" was partially regulated.

It would seem unlikely that this infant had been able to conceptualise mother, form a stable image of her or was now undergoing a grief reaction in any way comparable to that of an adult. Attempts to conceptualise the mental processes of infancy are speculative, but nevertheless important to an understanding of infantile grief.

Concepts about death in infancy and childhood have been reviewed by Maurer (1966), Sekaer (1987), Wass (1984), and Furman (1984).

Piaget (1973) described the sensorimotor stage of cognitive development, which lasts from birth to around two years of age, in which the individual is mostly concerned with the senses and motor development, has limited language ability, no conscious thinking, and no concept of reality. Disappearance of an object or person is equated with that object ceasing to exist. If mother leaves the room, she is not there, no longer exists and there is not a concept of "mother being next door." It has been suggested that a stable mental representation of mother does not exist in the infant, who is said to lack object constancy. This would result in a very modified decathexis of that object if that object is lost, resulting in a modified mourning reaction. However, there is evidence to suggest that from a very early age the infant recognises its mother's face and breasts visually and responds with increased arousal and distress when confronted with a stranger.

It is unlikely that the young infant has any concept of death or dying, although "mother not there" could be synonymous with "no mother," which would increase physiological arousal, as mother buffers the infant from unpleasant alterations in environmental stimuli and provides gratifying nutrition. The cry of a newborn baby is an unconditioned reflex in response to sudden environmental changes, but this cry soon becomes conditioned to the "no mother" noxious stimulus, and the cry acts as a signal to the mother to attend to the baby, thus reversing the noxious stimulus.

Klein (1948) has analysed young children and psychotic adults and formulated hypotheses about the mental life of the infant in the first few months of life. She believed that the infant and young child mourned losses connected with feeding and weaning and went through phases of depression. The infant experienced anxiety as a result of its own destructive (unconscious) fantasies towards its mother (or usually parts of mother), which involved splitting, projection, and introjection. These fantasies could be activated by mother not being available, leaving the room or, presumably, dying. The way that the infant responded influenced the way in which loss in adulthood was responded to. Bowlby (1979) regarded her hypotheses as being unsatisfactory, but favoured the concept of loss in infancy or childhood leading to mourning in which aggression, which attempted to achieve reunion, was a powerful component.

The infant soon discovers its own fingers and limbs, finds that it can initiate movements which are a source of interest and delight and begins to distinguish its own body from the environment around. A parallel process has been suggested in which there is a lack of distinction between the "self" and the "other" or an undeveloped "ego boundary." This "symbiotic" or fused situation, in which the infant presumably regards its mother as an extension of itself has been discussed with regard to separation and individuation by Mahler (1972). For the young infant who is awake and not lost in pleasant reveries, a sudden perception of absence of mother could be experienced as an absence of part of the self, which could lead to an experience akin to (or the basis of) existential anxiety.

However, it is conceptualised in terms of psychological theory, perception by an infant of an absent mother (or absent surrogate) may be distressing, particularly in the dark, in an unfamiliar environment, if there are unexpected alterations in levels of stimulus intensity (such as loud noises or flashing lights) or if the infant is experiencing discomfort through fatigue, hunger, cold, or pain. The distress is communicated by crying, tears, physical movements of the limbs, a startled facial expression, or grimacing and closure of the eyes and sometimes an agitated visual search for a familiar face. The behaviour is terminated by physical or sometimes visual contact with the mother or surrogate, while, if there are additional provoking factors leading to discomfort, as listed above, they may require reversal. The cry of the lonely infant summons help from the mother or from other members of the tribe, which results in a diminution in environmental danger.

Bowlby (1977), who developed his ideas from psychoanalysis and ethology has addressed the concepts of bonding, reactions to loss and "separation anxiety" in the infant and child. The above scenario with an infant separated from its mother is a prototypical situation leading to separation anxiety. He regarded the need for closeness to a maternal figure which he described as "attachment behaviour," as being a primary drive of equal importance to the drives for food and sex, with equal implications for survival of the individual and species. Bonding to a maternal figure has parallels in other species and occurs at a critical period in development, and distress results if premature separation from that figure occurs. If the infant is not reunited with its caretaker, the protest phase eventually subsides, and if no substitute is provided, withdrawal, impairment of physical growth and failure to thrive result (Spitz, 1945).

Bowlby (1980) suggested that from seven to seventeen months, the infantile response to loss had some resemblance to that of the adult, the resemblance increasing as the child matured further. He described the reactions (1979) of children from fifteen to thirty months who were separated from the mother-figure in residential nurseries or hospitals based on his own and other studies, and described three phases, characterised as those of protest, despair, and detachment. The phase of protest often lasted for several days, accompanied by tears, anger, and demands for mother, to then merge into a phase of despair with withdrawal (which sometimes alternated with hope) to be followed by a stage of detachment, in which the mother was forgotten and was no longer of interest, even when she reappeared. These studies focused on reactions to time limited separations from the mother, in which the child was often placed in an unfamiliar environment.

Bereavement may involve a different set of social dynamics from the maternal separations described by Bowlby and medium to long-term outcome may differ accordingly.

Furman (1984) described two children who lost their mothers at ten weeks and four weeks respectively, who appeared to have no conceptualisation of death:

> "May was 10 weeks old when her mother died suddenly. She was first cared for by her grandmother, then by her aunt and, during her second year, by another aunt. May's many difficulties included frequent stomach aches, obesity, and a pervasive inability to feel good." (p. 199) "Sandra's mother died suddenly 4 weeks after Sandra's birth. The maternal grandmother at once assumed full care of Sandra, supported by the father and grandfather. In spite of her grief and the burden of her unexpected task she helped the baby overcome her immediate distress and enjoyed her unfolding development. When Sandra began to notice pictures of the dead mother, grandmother said "That's your Mommy." Following Sandra's first birthday, the anniversary of her daughter's death reactivated Mrs. A's mourning. Sandra was quite concerned about grandma's changed mood and occasional tears. She patted her and laughed in an effort to cheer up grandma. The latter gave Sandra a special hug and explained. "Sandra is a good girl. Grandma loves Sandra. Grandma cries for Sandra's dead Mommy. I'll be

OK." This relieved Sandra as she sensed grandmother's empathy and reassurance. The words, though not understood at the time, formed a valuable basis for later ways of communicating." (p. 200)

The importance of the availability of a mother (or substitute) to provide a nurturing, accepting agency which buffers the internal and external stresses on the infant should be emphasised, and loss of this, whether as a result of maternal death, illness, or diversion elsewhere, has adverse effects on the developing infant. Furman (1984) suggested that the bereaved infant may be affected by a change of mood in other family members. Infants sometimes sensed a family's periodic distress around anniversaries, picked up clues from photographs, and puzzled why certain relatives were missing. Temporary regressions in development (including the loss of verbal skills) and developmental arrests, which lead to maladjustments and symptom formation of a psychosomatic or neurotic type, have all been described.

The "normal" grief reaction in infants has not been extensively researched systematically and while the toxic effects of maternal loss and subsequent gross deprivation or abuse in early infancy have been described in some individual cases, the bereaved infant of less than six months can often switch its allegiances with relative ease to a substitute caretaker, provided it has adjusted to the different milieu, and the substitute caretaker is compatible. A profound emotional and cognitive allegiance to a specific mother may not develop fully until the brain of the infant has matured sufficiently to allow some degree of visual pattern recognition and the ability to maintain object constancy. However, in the one- and two-year-old separated children discussed by Bowlby (1979), grief, crying, and yearning for a specific mother clearly occurred.

THE GROWING CHILD— THE PREOPERATIONAL AND CONCRETE STAGES

The preoperational stage of cognitive development, described by Piaget (1973), lasts from approximately two to seven years of age. The child begins to utilise symbols and language to represent internal and external events and it then becomes possible to express fears, attitudes, and conflicts about death, and to verbalise grief. Logical thinking has not developed but is animistic (attributing life to inanimate objects, in a similar way to early forms of religion), magical, and artificalistic (believing that all objects in the world are manufactured to serve people), while there is an egocentric orientation in which there is a lack of differentiation between the internal and external worlds.

Nagy (1948) interviewed 387 Hungarian children from three to ten years of age and found that children under six often regard death as a continuation of life but, under different circumstances, as reversible, controlled by magic or fantasy, not happening to them or their families, or as a remote event and that it is prevented by good behaviour. These findings were confirmed by Koocher (1973). Anthony (1972) demonstrated that children from three years onwards ask questions about death, express fears about dying, and manifest anxiety when confronted with death.

Yalom (1980) reviewed the literature on the concept of death in children. He concluded that children discover death at an early age, consider the possibility of their life being extinguished, and then develop great anxiety as a result. This anxiety, he thought, was dealt with by denying the inevitability and permanence of death, manifested through myths suggesting immortality and through belief in a personal specialness, omnipotence, and invulnerability and in the existence of an ultimate rescuer. This denial is aided and abetted by protective adults. His contention restated appears to be that the young child has an initial, albeit primitive concept of death and personal annihilation, but is so fearful, that realistic concepts of death are rapidly denied and fantasies of immortality and rescue are put in their place. However, by adolescence, this denial is no longer effective, and with the greater resources available it is possible to face the inevitability of death. Whilst this pattern fits neatly with a supposition of basic inherent existential anxiety from early infancy, which is initially denied and then confronted subsequently, it may not correspond with the pattern of many children who do not encounter an early existential crisis and then utilise denial, but rather acquire their knowledge about and attitudes towards death in a stepwise or sporadic fashion.

The fantasies of immortality may be reinforced by parents who wish to spare a child's feelings, which was illustrated by Anthony (1972) in a conversation between a five year old child and his university professor mother:

Child: "Do animals come to an end too?"
Mother: "Yes, animals come to an end too. Everything that lives comes to an end."

Child: "I don't want to come to an end. I should like to live longer than everyone on earth."

Mother: "You need never die; you can live forever." (p 158)

Alternatively, the actions of an adult may instill a fear of personal annihilation in a child. A child psychiatrist colleague noticed that his children, aged three and five years, became very fearful of the household fly-swat after they had observed how effective it was at killing flies. The five-year-old daughter expressed a fear of dying like the flies if she came too close to it.

The child's wishes for immortality may be reflected in the popularity of stories such as James Barry's "Peter Pan" in which Peter never grew up, and children could reverse the death of the fairy, Tinkerbelle, by clapping.

Death in this stage of development is not usually regarded as final or irreversible and it is also difficult for the child to anticipate secondary changes in relationships and attachments, so the experience of grief following bereavement is modified accordingly. If a young child does not really believe that mother has died, but will reappear if wished for hard enough (an example of magical thinking), then a grief reaction may not occur in the same way as in an older child or adult. However, despite the limited concepts and knowledge of death by children in the preoperational stage, they ask questions, are puzzled, try to correlate the observable data into their cognitive "map," but are often unable to do this, so resort to a magical explanation or ignore the situation. The corresponding emotional reactions may be of initial protest (Bowlby, 1979) often manifested by increased aggression. Wolfenstein (1969) regarded the rage reaction as the commonest form of bereavement reaction in children and adolescents. Despair, yearning, and clinging behaviour to an alternate caretaker may subsequently occur, while some children develop phobic symptoms and become more readily distressed by situations with which they would have previously coped. Early exposure to death of a secondary object such as a relative, friend, or pet may assist the child to develop increased knowledge about death and the feelings engendered. For children who have been brought up on a farm, birth and death may be everyday phenomena which familiarise the young child to these events. The young child may respond with apparent indifference to the death of a relative or neighbour with whom he or she has no close attachment, but given older role models of parents who are mourning, he may mimic adult responses, which are socially acceptable.

The four-year-old child may be filled with curiosity over the mechanics of the burial, what it is like being in a coffin, what happens when the worms get in, and demand to know the answer in situations embarassing to adult by-standers.

Oversimplified concepts or inadequate explanations about a family death may present the child with awesome situations. A child of six years who was referred to a psychiatrist colleague with a fear of going out of the house after the death of his father was simply frightened that "the hand of God" would come out of the sky and "take him away" as, so, he had been told, had happened to his father. A girl of four years who refused to go on holiday and became very distressed explained that grown ups told her that her dog, Sam, had "gone on holiday," when she had seen him killed under the wheels of a truck. "Going on holiday" was therefore synonomous with being run over by a truck.

Nagy (1948) described children from the ages of five to nine who "personified" death as a phantom figure, like the "Grim Reaper," who is the cause of death. Death was avoidable if capture by this figure was avoided, but once caught, death was reversible.

Piaget (1973) described the stage of concrete operations from approximately seven to eleven years of age in which thinking is no longer egocentric, but becomes logical. The concept of conservation, of mass, weight, and volume, which marks the end of the era of magical thinking, has developed by the end of the pereoperational stage. Real objects, the "concrete" are of more interest than the abstract. The concepts of reversibility (in arithmetic), classification, and seriation (organising objects into ordered series such as increasing size) emerge. With the emphasis on the concrete, the natural, and the observable, the child attempts to discover what differentiates life from death. Death is now understood as irreversible, although one may come back through resurrection, reincarnation, or other religious phenomena. Semantic definitions of death, e.g., "death is the end of living" and concrete explanations of why people die, e.g., "they get killed by rat poison" or "they die of cancer" (Wass 1984) predominate. Anthony (1972) demonstrated the ability to define the word "dead" by the age of seven years. Concepts about death, the Grim Reaper, possibilities of life after death, and bodily decay are culture-dependent.

Examples of bereavement reactions in children referred to by Furman (1984) and Sekaer (1987) appear to be usually of patients referred for treatment with problems ranging from sleep difficulties to learning difficulties, persistent soiling, and delayed development. Savin (1987) gave an example of an eight-year-old girl from a disturbed family who was already in treatment when her mother was murdered. Wolfenstein (1969) discussed the treatment of a four-year-old boy whose father suicided. These examples may not give a representative picture of bereavement reactions in childhood.

Sibling death in childhood may have important repercussions in family dynamics and the attitude to "survivor children" who may become endowed with qualities of the deceased. Krell and Rabkin (1979) described three identifiable types of family dynamics and survivor children, including the silent, guilty family in which the survivor child is characterised as "haunted," the overprotective family in which the child is "bound," and the family in which the major theme is of substitution and the child becomes "resurrected."

THE ADOLESCENT— ## THE STAGE OF FORMAL OPERATIONS

Piaget (1973) described the stage of formal operations which develops in adolescence and extends into adulthood. Logical reasoning about abstract ideas, hypothetical and deductive thinking, and a greater complexity of knowledge occurs, with an interest in ethics, politics, and religion, which result in a wide range of attitudes towards death and being. The grief reaction in adolescence bears more resemblance to that of the adult than to that of the child.

Nagy (1948) in her study of concepts of death found that after the age of nine years, they started to develop the adult concept of the irreversibility of death. Conflicts develop in the adolescent who is trying to establish his own adult identity and gain some independence when he loses a parent. He is then unable to deal adequately with his grief if he feels guilty about resentment towards that parent prior to the death. Unresolved mourning in adolescence may present as antisocial behavior including drug abuse, truanting, or promiscuity.

Wolfenstein (1969) described cases of bereaved adolescents who developed aggressive outbursts, suicide attempts, facial tics, homosexual/lesbian fantasies, and self-destructive behaviours, which she regarded as maladaptive reactions. She found rage, rather than grief, to be the dominant affect. The cases she described may have been unrepresentative, as they had been referred for treatment although increased disturbances in behaviour have been suggested by Rutter (1966) and Gregory (1965).

I observed a case of a sixteen-year-old boy, Peter, whose mother had died three years previously from terminal carcinoma. Father, a workaholic, who had not even begun to come to terms with his grief, remarried within the year. The grief of the family was not a subject for ventilation within the family. The stepmother, who was expected to be a replica of the deceased mother, found it increasingly difficult to cope with the expectations of the family, marital discord increased, and marital separation occurred within the first year of the marriage. An older sister had become pregnant by the time she was sixteen in a casual relationship, while a younger brother had become withdrawn and fallen behind a grade at school. Peter, an intelligent, good-looking youth, who had never had an opportunity to discuss or ventilate his feelings in a supportive environment, was then apprehended by police for stealing a sports car, driving it at high speed along a busy highway, and crashing it. Although initially placed in a juvenile detention centre, he stood out as being different from the other inmates who were largely recidivists from a delinquent subculture, and was referred for psychiatric assessment and treatment. Exploration of his mental state revealed a depressed, angry youth whose conflicts centred around the distress which mother had experienced and the difficulties that father had encountered in supporting the children emotionally, because of his own desperate avoidance of grief. Subsequent investigations confirmed that his acting-out behaviour resulted substantially from the family dysfunction relating to losses. Individual and family therapies with a focus on the expression of grief were utilised subsequently.

Family-based treatment approaches are beneficial in ameliorating long-term distress by promoting the natural resources of the family. Bentovim (1986) drew attention to this in bereaved children and emphasised the importance of aiding the expression of grief within the family.

For the adolescent whose involvement has switched from his family to the peer group, death of a friend may cause a severe grief reaction. Death of a friend in the pursuit of a hobby such as motorcycling or a political cause may result in idealisation of the deceased, with splitting and projection, so that the rest of the world or adults become imbued with undesirable and "bad" qualities, whereas the friend who died was "selfless and pure."

Podell (1989) described adolescents who were mourning the traumatic deaths of peers killed in a fire at an amusement park. Reactions including disbelief, dreams of their colleagues being incinerated, fears of their own death, vulnerability, sleep disturbance, abdominal pain, muscular tension and, commonly, identification with the victims, feeling dead, with no future, were expressed in group discussions. He drew attention to survivor guilt in adolescents which may be particularly prominent because of the specific phase of superego development through which they were going. The individual who has experienced unresolved traumatic loss earlier in childhood, may, with the increased resources of adolescence, be better able to work through losses subsequently and this was seen in the complicated grief reactions of some adolescents in this study. The lost peer may be identified with or seen as a self object, an extension and regulator of the adolescent's ego, which induced powerful feelings of loss of part of the self in some of the above individuals. The importance of the identification of the adolescent with a peer group may result in considerable grief when these bonds are disrupted.

A severe grief reaction may occur in the adolescent who has experienced falling in love for the first time, followed by a separation.

Wolfenstein (1969) described adolescents as undergoing a "sort of mourning" process, in the normal course of development, for early parental relationships which have to be relinquished to enable them to embark on the formation of nonincestuous mature adult relationships. Sugar (1968) considered that the adolescent was mourning for infantile objects from which he is separating in three phases of separation, namely, those of protest, disorganisation, and reorganisation.

"Altruistic mourning" in which there is a reaching out and feeling for others who share the bereavement (as well as an immersion in personal grief) may become possible in adolescence as a result of increasing empathy with others, without being bound to them in a symbiotic or incestuous mode.

THE STUDIES OF BEREAVED CHILDREN

There are no studies to date which have been able to directly assess nonclinical groups of bereaved children, using standardised assessment procedures, a control group, and base-line measures.

Raphael (1982) found in a clinical sample of thirty-five children aged from two to eight years a high rate of postbereavement behavioural disturbance initially which included high anxiety, exaggerated separation responses, clinging behaviour, excessive crying, marked aggressive behaviour, sleep disturbance, and disorders of eating and toileting.

Burns et al. (1986) surveyed families in which a sudden infant death syndrome had occurred. The families responding to a questionnaire indicated that of fifty children aged over two years (90% being less than six years), 54 percent grieved longer than one year and 40 percent grieved less than six months, which may have been a similar duration of grief to that described in adults.

Auslander (1987) reviewed the literature on bereavement research in Israel and concluded that children who lost their fathers in war showed clear evidence of emotional and behavioural problems, with possible evidence of changes in cognitive levels in which performance and ability levels were depressed.

Kaffman, Elizur, and Gluckson (1987) reviewed their own research with twenty five normal preadolescent kibbutz children who had lost their fathers during the 1973 war in Israel. Over 40 percent of this nonclinical sample displayed a wide range of severe emotional and behavioural postbereavement problems in a prospective study. The majority of children showed clear-cut grief reactions, with crying, moodiness, sorrow, and longing, while 54 percent displayed anger or protest reactions. In the majority, the sorrow, grief, and anger were expressed concomitantly with denial of the loss and a search for or attempt to revive the lost father. Nearly 50 percent experienced an increase in fears and phobias. Coping with trauma was sometimes achieved through reading sad books or writing, painting, and games related to the trauma. Two-thirds of the children developed increased dependency on their mothers. A marked diminution in grief tended to occur after 3½ years, although 39 percent still showed marked emotional impairment. It was concluded that in the kibbutz, as in other social structures, the death of father in early childhood was a crisis with long-term consequences. A comparison sample of twenty one city children raised in a traditional family framework revealed similar patterns of grief in both samples, although there was a higher frequency of overly dependent behaviour and night fears and a significantly higher prevalence of denial of death in the city children, which may have been related to some sociocultural differences between the city and the kibbutz. Bereavement reactions seemed to be influenced by pretraumatic variables such as the emotional status and personality, family discord, and separations and by posttraumatic variables such as the availability of a substitute father figure, mother's response to the loss and her relationship with the child.

A systematic, controlled study was conducted by Van Eerdewigh et al. (1982) who interviewed fifty widows and widowers in order to record the reactions of their children to the bereavement at one month and thirteen months after the death. Information on one hundred and five children ranging from two to seventeen years, with an average age of eleven years was compared with a group of controls. The interview included items about general adaptation to the death, school performance, behaviour problems, symptoms relevant to psychopathological manifestations and general health. The frequency of symptoms which were significantly increased in the bereaved children at some time during those thirteen months were crying (65%), sadness (52%), irritability (39%), temper tantrums (35%), withdrawal (31%), sleep troubles (19%), bed-wetting (19%), poor school performance (18%), and decreased appetite (15%). Sadness and crying tended to decrease over the thirteen months, while disinterest in school and abdominal pain increased over this time. Fighting siblings and general interests (which could be regarded as signs of normality) tended to increase. A minor form of depressive syndrome, defined on the presence of three depressive symptoms, persisted over the thirteen months (14% compared with 4% of controls), as did bed-wetting, while temper tantrums increased. There were no significant increases in behaviour problems nor severe forms of depression, nor was the general health affected. Overall there appeared to be little psychopathology in the year following bereavement, apart from an early dysphoria. There was a small (6%) nonstatistically significant group of severely depressed children, usually adolescent boys who had lost their fathers and who had a depressed mother.

Van Eerdewigh et al. (1985) examined the risk factors of sex and age in the above children and the sex and psychopathology of the surviving parents. Dysphoria, a widespread drop in school performance and withdrawn behaviour were significantly increased in bereaved children of both sexes and at all ages, while temper tantrums, bed-wetting, and the depressive syndrome only increased in the age and sex categories normally associated with those conditions. The minor depressive syndrome was seen predominantly among the bereaved children who were female and older. The younger bereaved children were mostly affected with temper tantrums, bed-wetting and loss of interest in activities. There was an unexpectedly higher rate of bed-wetting among bereaved females compared with bereaved males. The milder depressive syndrome was thought to be a specific reaction to the stress of bereavement, whereas it was unclear how the severer depressive syndrome was related to the bereavement. This white community sample which was only reviewed over a short term did not display the behavioural difficulties which have emerged in longer-term studies of an ethnically mixed clinic population such as those of Rutter (1966) or Gregory (1965). The loss of the same-sex parent did not emerge as an important factor in the development of psychopathology. In the short term for both boys and girls the loss of father resulted in higher average psychopathology than loss of mother. This psychopathology was more likely to be evident if mother was depressed. It was suggested that loss of father, who was usually a bread winner, had implications for the entire family both emotionally and economically.

The study of cognitive processes, affective changes, and fantasy in bereaved children, has usually been performed in the context of single patients referred for treatment who may not be representative of the bereaved child. The apparent absence of persistent adult mourning in the very young child has led analysts to question whether this occurs before adolescence.

DO CHILDREN MOURN?

This question has usually been posed by analysts in relation to the loss of the primary object in childhood. Sekaer (1987) has reviewed opinions on the capacity of children to mourn and the form which this takes. Bowlby (1979) has taken an interest in mourning processes in young children and regards them as occurring, but on an abbreviated time scale, and involving a process leading to detachment which develops prematurely (in comparison with adults). This masks a strong residual yearning for and anger with the lost person. He believed that the anger and yearning persisted at an unconscious level but sometimes emerged and would tend to be regarded as pathological in older children and adults.

The debate would be clarified by a definition of mourning in childhood, which Sekaer (1987) attempted. Freud (1957) described mourning as a process involving the gradual relinquishment of the libidinal tie to a mental representation of the lost object through a painful process of decathexis carried out by repeatedly confronting memories of the lost one with the reality of the loss. While that definition might be appropriate in mature individuals who have a clear mental representation, are able to tolerate pain, and have had many experiences of separating reality from fantasy, it would be less appropriate in a child who had not yet developed these qualities. A simpler definition of mourning with clinical value would be that it is the process of mental work following the loss of a loved one, usually through death. Sekaer (1987) pointed out that the identification and decathexis which occur in adult mourning vary in form in the child depending on his developmental level. She pointed out the need for a substitute in a bereaved child, the need to work through feelings associated with loss, fantasies of an imaginary parent which may be a creative solution to loss, and the need to work through the significance of a loss as the child passes through subsequent developmental stages.

Spitz (1946) and Anna Freud (1960) both queried the concept of mourning in infants and young children although the latter considered that the young child was capable of a mourning reaction as early as two or three years of age.

Wolfenstein (1966) considered that children prior to adolescence underwent an "adaptation reaction" which was not the same as mourning, in that there is not the same decathexis of the lost parent prior to the cathexis of a new object. There is no hiatus in attachment, rather a transfer of an attachment almost immediately, or an intensification of an attachment already in existence, such as the strengthening of an attachment to a grandparent or surviving parent.

Robert Furman (1964) and Erna Furman (1974) described bereaved children who appeared capable of mourning in the phallic and anal sadistic stages respectively. Furman (1984) considered that both "detachment," which involved intense memories and longing and identification, an unconscious process, which involved taking on some aspects of the dead loved one, occurred in bereaved children, the phase of detachment being aided in young children by concrete reminders of the deceased such as photographs and possessions.

Lopez and Kliman (1979) described a girl who lost her mother at nineteen months of age and subsequently at the age of four years showed an intense ambivalent tie to her dead mother, but was able to work through and resolve this, transferring her libido to her grandmother.

The child needs parents to look to, to idealise, to model himself on and to protect him. He cannot fully accept the loss of his parents either through death or separation, cannot conceptualise death anyway until the stage of concrete operations, may not have the ability to verbalise his distress in early childhood, so resorts to anger, denial of the loss or fantasies about his parents being alive in another place or returning. The possibility of a hiatus in his primary relationship is intolerable so a substitute primary attachment is made to a suitable figure as soon as possible, and if there is not a suitable person available, to a fantasied parent. This differs from the bereaved adult in whom there is often a gap of months or years before a new attachment is formed.

Savin (1987), in discussing the ability of the child to mourn, emphasised the degree of maturity, the ability to understand the concept of death, the degree of attachment to the deceased loved one, the existence of a realistic concept of death, the ability to tolerate and express longing, the presence of a surviving parent or a parent substitute, and a freedom from excessive anxiety.

The form that mourning takes varies depending on the developmental stage. Persistent denial, openly expressed rage at the deceased or a noncomprehension of death, which may all be regarded as pathological in the bereaved adult could be regarded as normal manifestations of mourning in the child. Nevertheless partial or intermittent denial, some anger towards the medical profession, and hallucinatory phenomena about the deceased are all common accompaniments of the adult grief reaction.

Assumptions about the young child (that he should not attend the funeral, nor be exposed to the grief of adults, that he cannot understand anything about death) may on occasion be the misplaced projections of well-intentioned adults, who would like themselves to be shielded from the effects of bereavement. The apparent blocking of a mourning reaction in a child may be in response to such a situation.

The manifestations of childhood grief may parallel those of depressed children, in that dysphoric, irritable, or withdrawn behaviour alternates with apparently normal interludes of play. This may be an effective means of distraction following bereavement in order to encounter the problem of loss from a fresh perspective and with renewed affective resilience.

The dramatic symptoms of hallucinatory type, usually of the deceased in a visual mode, have been described in bereaved adults by Parkes (1986). These have also been described in three nonpsychotic children by Yates et al. (1988), one being a twelve-year-old girl who hallucinated her dead stepfather, six months postbereavement; another, a nine-year-old boy who had an imaginary companion, following the stillbirth of a brother seven years previously; and the other, a fourteen-year-old depressed girl who hallucinated a dead great-grandmother. Although other complex factors had impinged on these children, it was proposed that these phenomena had arisen from incomplete mourning in a closely bound mother-child dyad and fulfilled individual and family needs.

We can conclude that children's grief reactions are not dissimilar to those occuring in adults and can best be understood in terms of their developmental stage, knowledge of death, and social milieu. The adult, however, differs from the child in that he is more cognisant of the reality and irreversibility of death, is more socialised, with prescribed rituals to guide him in his responses, is often more familiar with the emotions associated with loss, and is more practised at controlling, suppressing, or working through them. The internal mental work that proceeds in the bereaved child, while not identical to that of the adult and difficult to quantify, could reasonably be regarded as the mourning of that child.

ADULTHOOD

Normal and pathological grief will be discussed in detail in the relevant chapters. A brief overview of young, middle, and late adulthood follows.

Young adults are developing closer nonincestuous adult relationships, some of them intimate. They may be concentrating on pursuing a career, starting a family, and developing active recreations or hobbies. While establishing these relationships, separations and divorce may lead to intense grief. Untimely death of peers from accident, suicide, or the diseases of young adults, such as AIDS and certain neoplastic conditions, may create considerable conflict in the bereaved. Bereavements may be experienced in the context of work, recreation and in battle zones. Ageing relatives may be dying, which, although predictable, may not be anticipated and may represent the loss of very early relationships. The realisation of the inevitability of death amongst young adults begins to emerge.

Miscarriage, stillbirth, death of infants, and young children may be particularly traumatic to hopeful parents. In the developing world the frequency of these deaths is high and epidemics confront total populations with the possibility of frequent bereavements. Women may be more intimately affected in these bereavements than men and have a higher awareness than men of the possibility of mishaps.

Yalom (1980) reviewed the research on death anxiety in adults which consists of a number of fears about one's personal death including its effect on others, the possibility of pain in dying and the experiences which may follow death. He concluded that there was some evidence of a positive correlation between high death anxiety and depression, neuroticism, early loss or lack of religious belief, that it increased as one moved from conscious to unconscious experience, that the fear of death increased in the aged if psychologically immature, or if there were few life activities to engage in. He emphasised that death anxiety which is consciously acknowledged may not reflect that at an unconscious level. Anxieties about death if not confronted lead to psychopathology including further anxiety.

Death anxiety of a severe form or thanatophobia has been discussed by Wahl (1959). He pointed out how rarely it had been discussed as a clinical entity in the literature, in spite of its frequency in practice. It occurs not infrequently as part of a panic disorder, in which an individual has symptoms of palpitations, giddiness, sweating, and fears of a severe physical illness and imminent death. Most sufferers from this disorder, after careful assessment by a physician, are reassured that they are not in danger of immediate death, and the symptoms may be treated both psychologically and pharmacologically. However, it may be found sometimes in individuals suffering from major depressive disorders with psychotic features in which convictions of terminal disease and dying sometimes occur and they are not so easily reassured about the absence of physical illness until antidepressant treatment has been commenced.

A sexual difference in death anxiety was upheld in a study by Thorson and Powell (1988) of 599 adolescents and adults which demonstrated that death anxiety (about the complications of one's own death), as measured on a 25-item death anxiety scale, was higher in women than men and that women were also more concerned about bodily decomposition and feared pain.

The young adult is not always well equipped psychologically to deal with death or bereavement. An expectation in the twentieth century of medical technology prolonging life indefinitely is common, while young adults often assume that they are invulnerable and deny a possibility of personal death until much later. At this stage the adult is usually unprepared for the possibility of bereavement and its effects. Rearing children or busy involvement in other activities or careers does not always allow adequate time for grieving. Western society does not allow much time for nor provide sufficient ritual framework for the expression of grief, so that the young adult, who is concerned with other things, may not be given many opportunities or encouragement to grieve in a social setting.

During early to middle adulthood there is an increasing realisation of personal mortality. Jaques (1965) described the "mid-life crisis" which occurred from thirty-five years of age and involved a growing conscious realisation of the certainty of the personal death and an associated reworking of the infantile experience of loss and grief. Around this time, creativity (manifested more obviously in creative artists, but present in all of the population) altered dramatically, either ceasing or altering in its form, which he linked with the realisation at a conscious level of ultimate death. To weather the mid-life crisis it was necessary to come to terms with internal hate and destructiveness and the inevitability of death.

Further losses may include those of children who are becoming independent and leaving home, retrenchment, or financial losses which may all entail grief.

As the adult ages, the experience of bereavement of family members, particularly parents and friends, confronts him with the inevitability of his own demise. Loss of physical health or vigor, declining cognitive functions, loss of status within the community, loss of certain roles, or retirement may all be followed by grieving and compound the effects of a bereavement. Eric Erikson (1963) in describing the life cycle drew attention to the fear of death which arises in the final stage of maturity (the stage of ego integrity versus despair) in the individual who has not achieved a sense of satisfaction that he has lived a productive life.

Butler (1963) suggested that older adults reach a resolution of anxieties with regard to death, undergoing a life review and perhaps finding some meaning in death. This was supported in a study by Thorson and Powell (1988) utilising a death anxiety scale, which also revealed that the older respondents were concerned over the existence of an afterlife and loss of personal control.

Familiarity with repeated experiences of personal loss and bereavement may diminish the impact of grief. However, in some individuals each bereavement is accompanied anew by the same pain. Coping mechanisms which arise in the elderly may involve philosophical or religious detachment or seeking distraction through vicarious identification with the pleasures of the younger generations. Sharing grief experiences may be a useful way of coping, although grief is sometimes deemed to be too personal for this to happen. Anticipatory mourning, which involves the working through of some feelings prior to an expected loss, and making realistic provisions for the future would both buffer the effects of a loss. The lusty protest of the infant separated from its mother has changed almost beyond recognition in the bereaved elderly adult to a sadly resigned yearning.

PLAYING, DEATH, AND LOSS

A major activity of the child, which may be preparing him for the tasks of adulthood, or may be an instinctual activity without purpose, is play. It appears likely that perceptual, motor, cognitive, and social skills can all be practised in play. I discussed the relationship between play and humour (1988), both of which may be utilised to express, control, or alleviate anxiety.

Death and its imponderables and the possible loss of close figures arouses anxiety. Death of the self or nonbeing is potentially frightening. The child explores these areas and learns to control anxiety through play.

The infant learns about not-being and being through the simple game of peek-a-boo (old English—dead or alive). I suggested (1988) that this game could prepare the infant for separations and assist him in gaining control of the appearance and disappearance of those around. The positive, pleasurable emotions engendered by reappearance of his mother counteracted the increase of anxiety levels associated with her disappearance. The infantile game of throwing away objects for admiring bystanders to retrieve has been discussed by Maurer (1960) with reference to being there and not being there, with an eventual concept of "all gone" when finally the bystander tires of picking up the object. This notion is also reinforced when objects are flushed down the toilet or sink outlet or thrown in the garbage bin, which may activate fears by the infant of being disposed of in a similar way himself, but becomes a game when he learns how to activate the process by pressing a button.

The toddler begins to encounter nursery rhymes which have associations with disease and death, although he does not always appreciate these:

Ring-a-ring of roses,
a pocket full of posies.
A-tissue, a-tissue,
all fall down!

This rhyme, sung by children holding hands in a ring may have referred originally to the symptoms of the bubonic plague, in which the ring of roses represented the cutaneous manifestations, the pocket full of posies indicated the glandular enlargement, "a-tissue" was the sneeze indicating respiratory involvement and falling down, the rapid death. Leavesley (1984) suggested that the rhyme was originally written to remind the citizenry of the efficacy of sweet smells in preventing pneumonic plague.

The rhyme "The Bells of St. Clements" ends with the line "and here comes the axeman to chop off your head" which is gleefully chanted by children, who playfully imitate the axeman.

Fairy stories rich in fantasy, symbolism, and animistic concepts involve death, sometimes violent, and reincarnation for those who are good. This matches the preoperational stage and introduces the concept of dying. However, by the stage of concrete operations, the child has moved away from the fairy stories which occurred "once upon a time" to stories about the present and future, in which death is encountered, often in a matter-of-fact way, but extended descriptions of grief do not usually occur, although vengeance may be sought for the death of a friend. Some stories written for prepubescent and pubescent girls focus on the death of a ballet star or favourite horse, which is responded to with grief on losing what has become an idealised object. Children in the latency period enjoy ghost and murder stories which provoke fear, but in a safe environment and begin to raise more questions about death and the after-life.

Television exposes children to death, sometimes violent, in news programs as well as in drama. Isolated viewing may be inappropriate for children, who require parental (or adult) guidance and input. The fiction that the actors on cowboy films never really die in gunfights but reappear the following week to fight another battle may shape unrealistic (and sometimes antisocial) attitudes. Horror films may be of fascination to the child in the later stage of concrete operations but at an earlier stage could be disturbing. Humor may be utilised to approach the anxiety-provoking topic of death:

"It's not the cough that carries you off
It's the coffin they carry you off in."

In the adolescent, black humor about death or corpses can trivialise the topic of death, or "humanise" it.

Action games which introduce concepts about death include "cowboys and indians," "cops and robbers," and war games. At an earlier age, hide and seek and blind man's bluff introduce possibilities of disappearance and not being which are overcome by searching.

Role enactment games in which roles and situations are fantasised, such as "kings and queens", families and hospitals, involve the occasional possibilities of death, illness, and separations. A child of four years may spontaneously "pretend" to be dead, after asking what people do when they die.

Team sports and other competitive games, which extend into adulthood, involve a struggle in which one side is victorious and the other side defeated (and may be symbolically killed). However, the defeated opponent is always given another chance to "play," so that the "death" is reversible.

Death is defied in the amusement park in which participants ride on switch-backs, wheels and what appear to be dangerous pieces of machinery, whilst the ghost train and haunted house enable "jesting" with the spirits and the underworld, both of which bolster fantasies of personal immortality.

Children who have experienced a bereavement may undergo an alteration in their patterns of play. The young child may become more aggressive, more active, and alternate this with withdrawal and sadness, or have more difficulty in interacting with peers. The family in mourning may disapprove of play, while a serious atmosphere may inhibit the child from his normal pursuits. The bereaved toddler may play with dolls which "go away," "go to hospital," "are hurt," or he may actively attack his toys. Houses may be kicked down, while his preoccupations and mood are reflected in drawings. If there is a regression he may adopt more infantile mannerisms, with increased clinging, put objects in his mouth, and be less coordinated in motor skills. His major channel of expression may be in the form of play, although to facilitate these expressions about grief, an interested participant-observer may be required.

Creative outlets in bereaved children include the development of imaginary companions, who become reliable and regular playmates and imaginary parents. Sekaer (1987) considered that the imaginary parent could often be adaptive, allow a slow stepwise separation from the lost object, be temporarily utilised as a substitute object, and diminish loneliness. However, it could also be endowed with primitive qualities. There was often strong external pressure to keep the imaginary parent secret. She suggested that the later use of creative channels in adulthood may stem from an early parental bereavement and the initial use of an imaginary parent, imaginary companions and transitional objects.

Playing is not entirely the domain of the child. Competitive games are a source of pleasure to adults. The areas of creative fantasy, akin to play in which adults indulge include the visual arts, literature, drama, films, and music. In all of these areas separation and death can be portrayed, grief can be reenacted, and reminders of past and anticipated bereavement stimulate the cognitions and affects of the audience. Adults may leave the cinema with tears in their eyes, this confirming a moving, entertaining, or uplifting experience, and derive strength from identifying with the actors in their portrayal of grief.

The death of an individual may be celebrated by the wake, which is a party held in the presence of the corpse, or, more commonly, after the funeral in some Western cultures. The guests, in addition to offering their formal condolences to the bereaved and paying tribute to the departed may relax, sometimes joke, and toast the departed. This could be regarded as a form of playing, which helps to re-create a situation in which the deceased *could* be enjoying the party and listening to the adulations and jests about himself, and helps to further the mourning process in which memories and affects about the deceased are beginning to be stimulated and reviewed in a social setting. Haig (1988) discussed the role of the joking partner at funeral ceremonies in certain non-Western cultures.

Chapter 10

THE LOSS OF A PARENT IN CHILDHOOD

The sapling requires water, air, and light, the support of the soil for its roots, protection from the buffeting winds, and the warmth of the spring and summer to grow to maturity. The needs of the developing child are more complex and the parents' nurturance, support, and understanding interaction are required for the child to achieve emotional maturity and stability. The separation of the child from its parents, whatever the cause, is potentially disruptive to psychological development and could possibly result in psychopathology. However, the personality traits of the individual child, alternative sources of support, and other ameliorating factors such as peer interaction can modify both short- and long-term grief reactions. In the child who has a relationship with an abusive or noncaring parent, separation could be potentially beneficial, given a good foster parent and a possibility for expressing and working through conflicts. However, even an abusing parent can be viewed by the child as providing some security and be the principal attachment figure, so that separation anxiety and grief could be engendered initially when the child loses the figure.

Grief reactions and the modes of mourning in children have been considered in Chapter 9 on Grief and Development.

We now focus on childhood bereavement and its association with subsequent psychopathology when that child grows up into an adult.

CHILDHOOD BEREAVEMENT
AND ADULT PSYCHOPATHOLOGY

Childhood bereavement and loss have both been regarded as potent pathogenic situations in the causation of adult psychopathology although systematic research has not always confirmed initial impressions based on clinical experience. The initial task for researchers in this area is to establish what associations exist, if any, between childhood loss situations and the development of specific psychopathology in adults.

Finkelstein (1988) has reviewed studies in this area. There did not appear to be convincing evidence for an association between early loss and schizophrenia, but there was some evidence for an association between early loss and alcoholism, although this group may overlap with the depressives.

Krupnick (1984) drew attention to an apparently increased risk of physical and mental illness in adult life after parental death in childhood, with a suggested increase in incidence of physical distress, sexual identity impairments, difficulties with autonomy and intimacy, depression, suicide, and criminality. Such findings stir up the nature-nurture debate and provide potential evidence to apologists for diverse schools of psychotherapy.

Interesting findings have emerged from studies of adults with anxiety and mood disorders, although further research is required for clarification. Recent studies on anxiety disorders and mood disorders are outlined further below.

CHILDHOOD AND ADULT ANXIETY DISORDERS

Studies relating loss in childhood to subsequent adult anxiety disorders have not always distinguished types of loss, whether by death or separation.

Raskin et al. (1982) in the United States found that seventeen subjects with panic disorders (PDs) and sixteen with generalised anxiety disorders (GADs) reported a similar incidence of early separations from parents. It was not specified in this study whether parental bereavements were responsible for some of the loss situations.

A study which examined the relationship between separation experiences in children in different age groups and the subsequent development of adult depression, anxiety, or psychological morbidity was conducted by Tennant et al. (1982) in London. Separations occurring up to five years of age did not appear to affect the incidence of these conditions, but from five to ten years of age, separations caused by parental illness and marital discord were related to morbidity and in the latter instance were more likely to cause depression than anxiety in adulthood. The age at separation and the circumstances appeared to be particularly important in the subsequent development of psychopathology.

Faravelli et al. (1985) in an Italian study found that the rate of traumatic early life events in thirty-one agoraphobic patients with panic attacks was significantly higher than that in matched control subjects. Maternal separation, parental divorce and events occurring after the age of four years were significantly commoner in the agoraphobics. There was an increased incidence of parental death in childhood in the agoraphobic patients, but this was not statistically significant.

Torgersen (1986) compared thirty-two Norwegian patients with GADs with twenty-nine patients with PDs or agoraphobia with panic attacks. Patients with GADs more often experienced loss of either parent (through death or separation) before the age of sixteen years. Patients with PD or agoraphobia more often experienced chronic anxiety in childhood, suggestive of a genetic influence in these conditions, compared with a greater environmental influence in the GAD.

Bereavement in adolescence or early adulthood may be related to anxiety subsequently. Hafner (1987), in an Australian study, described an excess of paternal bereavement in fifty married female agoraphobic patients in childhood and early adulthood (before the age of thirty years). There was also a statistically significant excess of parental bereavement in a control group of nonagoraphobic psychiatric out-patients compared with the general population.

Tweed et al. (1989) conducted an epidemiological study of 3,803 persons in the United States. Childhood parental losses were found to be significant risk factors for anxiety disorders developing in adulthood, associations being demonstrated between early childhood maternal death and the subsequent development of agoraphobia with panic attacks and also between early childhood parental separation or divorce and agoraphobia with panic attacks or panic disorder. Possible explanations for these associations included disruption of attachment bonds, in terms of Bowlby's (1977) attachment theory and preseparation factors of a genetic or family dynamic origin which contributed to both the separation and to the development of an anxiety disorder in adulthood. Postseparation factors included a poor relationship with a stepparent or a depressed divorcee parent with a subsequently impaired parenting capacity, which could presumably sow the seeds of an anxiety disorder in the child. This study, because of its size, appears to carry more weight than the smaller studies which have often contained a selected or unrepresentative sample. Separation and death have been examined separately in this study.

It is not unreasonable to conclude on the basis of the above studies from different centres that there is some evidence for a relationship between early parental separation or bereavement and an anxiety disorder subsequently in adulthood.

CHILDHOOD DEVELOPMENT AND ADULT MOOD DISORDERS

There has been considerable debate and some empirical evidence about an association between the death of a parent in childhood and the subsequent development of a depressive disorder in adulthood. Finkelstein (1988) in a review of the literature drew attention to findings which were contrasting, but pointed out that the most consistent findings appeared to indicate a relationship between early maternal death and later depression, particularly of a severe form. However, Tennant (1988) in reviewing the same area, concluded that there was no evidence that parental death was a significant risk factor for depression, although there was some evidence that child-parent separations may contribute to adult depression. He pointed out that many of the initial studies did not distinguish losses through death or through parent-child separation, contained selected samples, had no controlled groups, or had too many confounding variables.

Does loss of a parent in childhood increase the likelihood of a depressive illness later in life? An impression may be gained when interviewing or treating individual patients that they were very much affected by their losses in childhood, but the possibility then arises that the past is viewed in a gloomy and negative light by the depressed patient, or there may be a depressive flavored search for meaning by the patient in recollecting his previous history. We now examine a few of the studies which have highlighted important aspects of childhood loss and adult depression.

The seminal study by Brown et al. (1977), in London, demonstrated that loss of mother (either through death or separation) before the age of eleven years was associated with a greater risk of depression both in those who attended psychiatrists and also in those in a random community sample, whereas loss of a father (or sibling) before the age of seventeen was not associated with a greater chance of developing depression. Other vulnerability factors which also predisposed these predominantly working class women to depression included three or more children under the age of fourteen years at home, lack of a confiding marital relationship, and lack of employment. He distinguished between all types of loss and demonstrated that among the women who were patients, deaths experienced in childhood were associated with psychotic-like depressive symptoms whereas other types of past loss (through separation) were associated with neurotic-type depressive symptoms. He suggested that the psychotic's sense of abandonment and the neurotic's sense of rejection may arise from the different attitudes which develop in bereavement and separation. The bereaved may come to regard personal effort as being futile, death as irreversible, this sense of irreversibility extending to losses of any kind, whereas the child who has lost a parent through separation and knows them to be still alive may feel rejected and develop a lifelong expectation of failure, but with a less passive cognitive set than that of the bereaved. He also related the development of depression to feelings of hopelessness which become generalised.

The findings that the loss of mother before eleven years, three or more children at home, the lack of a confiding relationship and the lack of employment all predisposed to depression were confirmed by Roy (1978) in a matched controlled study of women in London referred to a psychiatric clinic. He also observed that 29.7 percent of the depressed women had lost their father compared with 16.6 percent of controls. Roy (1981) studied a group of Canadian adult depressives and found that 44.4 percent had sustained a parental loss before the age of seventeen years. In a matched controlled study with a group of nondepressed psychiatric in-patients, parental loss was found to be significantly associated with depression. In 1985 he examined childhood loss which he divided into parent-child separations which were a significant predictor of depression and parent deaths which were not.

Tennant et al. (1981) conducted a community survey in London and found that parental death in childhood bore no relationship to either psychiatric symptoms nor to patient status (attending a psychiatric clinic), although parent-child separations were significantly associated with patient status.

Parker et al. (1986) found that being a member of a lower social class was the most consistent predictor of depression in adulthood in seventy-nine women in Australia whose mothers had died during childhood. The sudden death of mother, the perception of family support as being deficient in the immediate postbereavement phase, a longer delay between the mother's death and the stepmother assuming a maternal role, and an inadequate replacement mother-figure were all associated with adult depression. These factors experienced by a child would all influence the continuity and quality of parental care available.

Breier et al. (1988) found that the risks of parent death in a depressed and a nondepressed group were not significantly different (61% and 76% respectively). It was found that the quality of childhood home life subsequent to the parental loss was the most powerful predictor of adult psychopathology in 80 percent of the subjects. It is noteworthy that this particular sample in the United States, who consisted of respondents to a newspaper article, appeared to have been educationally advantaged, 43 percent having completed graduate professional training, indicating a possible skew to a higher social class.

From the foregoing it can be seen that the association between loss of a parent in childhood and adult depressive illness subsequently is a complex matter, without a simple answer. The immediate circumstances of the loss, whether through death or separation need to be distinguished. In the studies in which death of a parent was distinguished from other forms of loss, the cause of death was not always identified. Death resulting from suicide, drugs, or risk-taking activities may be associated with a mental illness in the parent which then raises the question about a genetic vulnerability to that illness in the child who manifests the same disorder.

It has been suggested that the quality of care available after the loss is of great importance. In addition to an emotionally supportive environment, social and economic factors play a major role. Changes in life style, schooling, recreational activities, and diet could all effect the well-being and subsequent mental health of the child.

The retrospective nature of all the studies is a problem, as is the lack of knowledge of the preloss cognitive, emotional, and social functioning of the children.

THE IMPACT OF PARENTAL LOSS IN CHILDHOOD ON FUNCTIONING

Tennant (1988), while noting that prolonged separations due to family discord appeared to contribute to the development of adult psychopathology, pointed out that parental separation may be beneficial when it terminated earlier turmoil. The same point could be made about parental death, and, in some cases, the quality of care for the child could improve after the death of a chronically ill, demanding, or noncaring parent, with a positive effect on mental health. However, the situation in which a close relationship with a caring parent is disrupted without adequate replacement by a substitute, with no supportive figure with whom to work through the loss, would be regarded as a "pathoplastic" influence by most clinicians.

The quality of care or ability of the parent to provide on-going care may be influenced by socioeconomic and cultural factors. The current measures of social class or educational level are somewhat crude but do indicate whether the remaining parent is able to continue providing the same standard of living or material life style without major financial constraints. Cultural factors such as the presence of a social network or extended family would be potentially useful in providing support to the nuclear family which has lost a member. The skills, flexibility, and "attractiveness" of the family which has sustained a loss would influence its adaptation and the potential replacement of the loss parent.

The widow may be so immersed inwardly in grief, ambivalence, or worry over how to meet financial commitments that she is unable to give emotional support to a young child. The "older" daughter who may still be in her prepubertal years may be expected to take over some of the responsibilities of the parent who has died and may have the role of a "little mother" thrust on her and be expected to care for younger siblings. This scenario is probably more common in the working class family where the father is unable to absent himself from work. Alternatively, the son of a widow may be expected to behave as the "man about the house" at a time when he has not satisfactorily resolved his own oedipal conflicts or is not yet ready to assume the mantle of the adult male.

Thus the impact of the loss of a parent through death or separation is a complex situation with many psychological, social, and cultural variables, which effect the immediate (and probably longer-term) mental health of the child.

THE RECALL OF CHILDHOOD LOSS

The memory of a childhood bereavement may be manifested in different ways in adulthood. There may be an active recall, under conscious control, of earlier losses which may be accompanied by an affect of sadness or pain. Environmental cues, such as photographs, conversations, music, or smells may trigger off memories. If the bereavement occurred after the age of five years, total amnesia for the loss would suggest an abnormality of grief, as would intrusive waves of grief many years later. A loss in early childhood is unlikely to be clearly remembered, if at all,

and the screen memories which sometimes arise may have been modified by vivid descriptions by other family members. In the adult who is
amnesic for a childhood loss, unexplained feelings of panic or dysphoria
sometimes arise in situations in which reminders of the loss are present.
In such a situation, there is a reminder of the threat of abandonment and
the feelings of insecurity which occurred in the early childhood loss.
Occasionally, recall may occur subsequently during psychotherapy or
hypnotherapy.

THEORETICAL LINKS BETWEEN CHILDHOOD LOSS AND ADULT PSYCHOPATHOLOGY

To fully explore the theoretical mechanisms by which a traumatic
childhood loss could be causally related to a mental illness in adulthood would involve a comprehensive consideration of many schools of
psychology, psychotherapy, and sociology and is beyond the scope of
this book.

Psychodynamic theory focuses on arrested or incomplete mourning in
infancy or childhood, and a tendency to introject the lost object. This
theory was propounded by Freud (1957) in his paper on mourning and
melancholia. (This is considered in more detail in Chapter 3.) Attachment theory considers that the sense of security is derived from a period
of bonding at a critical stage to an attachment figure which, if disrupted,
predisposes to subsequent psychiatric disorders or problematic relationships and has some value in explaining the apparent increase in adult
anxiety disorders following childhood loss.

It is of interest to speculate on some physiological processes which
could be set in motion by loss. Breier et al. (1988) in a comparison study
of adults with and without psychopathology proposed that early trauma
(from an experience of parental loss) resulted in enduring alterations in
neuroendocrine functioning in those who developed psychopathology
subsequently. It is not inconceivable that early stress-related disturbance
in neurochemical, hormonal, or immunological functioning might have
a permanent effect on central nervous system functioning or structure.
Permanent alterations in patterns of functioning of neurophysiological
processes could result in a predisposition to the development of a range
of psychiatric disorders in adulthood.

POSITIVE OUTCOMES OF CHILDHOOD LOSS

There may occasionally be other positive outcomes of loss. It is of interest to observe that genius may be related to early parent death. An association between high I.Q. (greater than 155) and a three-fold increase in early parent death was reported by Albert (1971) while Eisenstadt (1978) noted that prominent individuals listed in the *Encyclopedia Britannica* had a more frequent incidence of early parental death. Woodward (1974), however, did not find that the percentage of scientists who lost a parent before the age of fifteen was significantly higher than the general population, during any period of recent history, although a high percentage of eminent scientists did lose a parent in childhood. Silverman (1974) in reviewing the area discussed the problems in personal interaction which may develop in those who experience loss of either parent, with a resultant withdrawal from human contacts and a replacement of these with the greater certainty and impersonality of the physical laws of science. Haig (1988) has drawn attention to the possibility that comedians find their inspiration from tragedy and this may follow childhood losses. Fisher et al. (1983) has found that the mothers of comedians tended to be nonnurturant and expected their offspring to "grow up" and not be childish. Loss of a parent, whether through divorce or death, could force a premature growth of the child, who may resort to coping strategies which are adaptive, creative, or may even reduce the likelihood of a psychiatric disorder in adulthood. Sekaer (1987) has suggested that adult creativity may arise from an early parental bereavement.

POSTSCRIPT

It is noteworthy that the majority of studies on childhood loss appear to have been conducted in largely Western-oriented societies. It would be fascinating to examine the association between loss and adult psychopathology in non-Western societies, which are characterised by traditional extended social support systems, or in societies in which childhood losses are more prevalent. Research of this nature would have major implications for the policy makers who are interested in the mental health of future generations who inhabit the most populated parts of the world.

Chapter 11

THE LOSS OF A BABY

SACRED
To
The
Memory
of
CATHERINE M. BARNETT
Who departed this life 11th November 1857
Aged 26 Days
A slumbering babe is sleeping here
to put us fresh in mind
that die we must and turn to dust
and leave the world behind

Epitaph on headstone,
Isle of the Dead, Tasmania

The loss of a baby or young child is a tragic event and a source of terrible grief to the parents. The mother who has borne a child, nurtured it, and invested her hopes for the future in that child may undergo a period of profound grief, with feelings of desperate yearning, emptiness, personal failure, guilt, and anger. It has been increasingly recognised that miscarriage and stillbirth may also engender severe grief reactions.

The medical and nursing professions have sometimes shied away from becoming too involved in these situations which do activate painful emotions, or have not always been aware of the course of grief which may follow such a loss. This, at times, has resulted in advice to the mother to avoid reminders of the dead fetus or stillbirth, to suppress grief, and to get on with her life as normal, which may be appropriate at a later stage of mourning but which is insensitive or may be untherapeutic at an early stage following the loss. This stance and the attempt by parents to replace a stillbirth with a viable infant has been questioned by Lewis et al. (1978). The tendency of society and the medical profession to "play down" the losses incurred by parents of young children and infants has been redressed in recent years following an increasing awareness of the normality of grief reactions and the importance of expressing them. There have been an increasing number of studies which have attempted to address the area systematically.

Raphael (1983) has skilfully drawn together the literature on parental loss and described the range of emotional reactions manifested by bereft parents.

Most studies have focussed on maternal grief. Several recent studies, including those by Theut et al. (1989), Dyregrov et al. (1987a) (1987b), Tudehope et al. (1986), and Nicholas et al. (1986), demonstrated that mothers experienced (and expressed) grief more deeply than did fathers, which would be consistent with clinical experience. The mother is initially more closely involved with the fetus and baby physically. Opportunities for the formation of attachment bonds arise more frequently between the mother and baby initially. Hormonal changes in the mother during and following pregnancy and the reflexes involved in breast feeding may also promote considerable emotional involvement with the baby. The attention of the father may be diverted to his employment or peers for some of the time which may also decrease the intensity of his attachment bonds to the infant, although with decreasing role differentiation between the sexes this could change, with fathers spending more time at home providing care to their off-spring while mother goes out to work.

While the physical closeness of the mother to her fetus and its movements and the physical changes associated with pregnancy act as a reminder of her growing baby, which promotes the initiation of healthy attachment bonds, the converse can occur if the baby is unwanted or the mother is ambivalent about the pregnancy. She may then harbor aggressive phantasies towards the baby. Following the loss of an unwanted pregnancy there may be feelings of relief, but alternatively there may be considerable guilt over the final realisation of the wished-for death.

Studies of bereaved parents following perinatal death indicate a deterioration in psychological health in many parents which sometimes persists for years and may be severe. Nicol et al. (1986) described a severe deterioration in health with psychological and related physical symptoms in 20 percent of their sample. Tudehope et al. (1986) found that 31 percent of families who lost a newborn infant eight weeks previously experienced major pathological effects. Dyregrov et al. (1987b, 1987c) found that the greatest anxiety and distress occurred in those parents who experienced a sudden infant death at home. Murray et al. (1988) found that parents who experienced a perinatal death were more depressed than the general population even several years after the death of an infant.

Immediate symptoms in the bereaved parents which were described by Tudehope et al. (1986) included sleep disturbance (51%), depression (34%), anorexia (33%), anxiety (19%), social withdrawal (18%), morbid preoccupation (9%) and guilt, anger or hostility (9%). These symptoms are similar to those found in grief reactions following the loss of a spouse. Dyregrov et al. (1987a) described anxiety, self reproach, sadness, intrusive thoughts about the child and sleep disturbance which occurred one to four years after the loss. Dyregrov et al. (1987b) drew attention to the anxiety for surviving and later born children experienced by bereaved parents. There appeared to be a fundamental change in the belief system of parents about the future security of the family. It was suggested that these parental reactions paralleled those following other extreme life events, in which a world, previously perceived as safe to live in, is transformed into a place of uncertainty, insecurity, and fear and the individual anticipates new disasters. I have observed this existential insecurity develop in parents who have experienced a sudden infant death and subsequently become very anxious and persistently fear for the safety of other children.

Other stress during pregnancy may be associated with a worse outcome following parental bereavement. Nicol et al. (1986) found that stressful events or a crisis during pregnancy predicted a worse or pathological outcome for parental bereavement. A bereavement or major loss during a pregnancy, followed by the loss of that infant, is particularly difficult to cope with.

It has been suggested that giving birth to a congenitally handicapped child is followed by the experience of grief, as the hoped-for perfect baby has not eventuated. Nicholas et al. (1986) compared the reactions of parents who gave birth to a congenitally handicapped child to those who experienced a crib death. The crib death parents experienced higher levels of unresolved grief.

The intensity of grief may be related to the stage of pregnancy. Although Peppers and Knapp (1980) concluded that there was no difference in the magnitude of the reactions to loss through miscarriage, stillbirth, or neonatal death, this study included some participants who were reporting experiences from thirty-six years previously. Nicol et al. (1986) found no

difference in the outcome of bereavement six to thirty-six months following either stillbirth, death of a neonate, single baby, or twins. However,
Theut et al. (1989), in their comparison of middle class parents who lost a
baby later in pregnancy (either through stillbirth or neonatal death)
with a loss earlier in pregnancy (through miscarriage), found that the
late loss group experienced more grief than the early loss group and
were also more likely to manifest unresolved grief during a subsequent
viable pregnancy. Dyregrov et al. (1987c) found that a stillbirth or
neonatal death was not associated with as much pathology as a sudden
infant death at home.

The management and support available to bereaved parents is of
importance. While age, socioeconomic status, and religious affiliation
were not demonstrably related to parental bereavement outcome by
Nicol et al. (1986), the perception of support by husband or family was of
great importance. The importance of support from hospital staff also
predicted higher levels of well-being (Murray et al., 1988). Tudehope et
al. (1986) discussed the desirability of contact with the baby around the
time of death. They concluded that observing but not holding or touching the dead baby could give rise to an abnormal or more severe grief
reaction in parents and this was confirmed by Nicol et al. (1986). It is
generally regarded that physical contact with the dead baby may be
important for subsequently resolving grief. Could it be that the sense of
touch is a more primitive sense which confirms the reality of a situation
at a deeper emotional level?

Interventions with bereaved parents may include those which might
be employed following bereavement of any close relationship. The opportunity to withdraw from the normal daily engagements and to ventilate
feelings of yearning, anger, or guilt may be essential. Help in initiating
the expression of grief may be of importance if grief has been delayed or
suppressed.

The situation is unlike the loss of an adult or older child in which
there has been time spent together during which a store of memories
have been established, some of which may be fondly treasured, others of
which require working through in order to loosen the affective bonds
and gain a perspective of a life which may be lived without the lost
person. There has been little time to build up memories, which are few.
Much of the investment of emotion has been in an anticipated person
with hopes and plans for his future. In some ways it is easier to grieve
over the loss of an individual who may be seen, felt, heard, and smelt,

rather than a mysterious, unseen, and unknown being onto whom is projected all sorts of phantasies by the bereaved parent. It may be of importance for the bereaved parents to have memories of the dead infant, such as a lock of hair, a photograph or the blanket he slept on, which may act as a focus to initiate grief. In order to bring home the reality of the loss it is sometimes important for the parents to have some contact with the stillborn infant. If there are gross abnormalities the parents may not wish to view the infant entirely, but see parts of the body which are normal, such as the limbs. It is possible for parents to feel the infant or hold it. It is generally thought that viewing, touching, or holding the dead infant may be followed by fewer pathological grief responses. Parents may frequently express guilt over the death, or alternatively find fault in medical or nursing delays or inadequacies. If the medical staff can help the parent through this period without becoming too defensive, it may be possible to relieve some of the burden of guilt. In the initial stages following the death, parents may be too numbed or shocked to adequately take in information of a complex nature, and it may be of importance for parents to discuss the details subsequently with informed medical or nursing staff in order for them to grieve adequately. The parents may require to idealise the child or stillbirth, e.g., "He was so peaceful and quiet." "She was a perfect baby," or may focus on the few early encounters in great detail, e.g., "He was smiling at me with his eyes," or "She was just beginning to recognise me." Parents should be encouraged to think about the possibilities for funeral arrangements.

It is important to realise that parents may not be in a good position to support each other having experienced a severe loss. Both parents may be so absorbed in their own grief that they are unable to pay much attention to the needs of the other. The manner of grieving may be very different between parents. No two individuals grieve in an identical manner. One parent may resort to religious comfort, while the other may feel a certain anger towards a God who can cut short an infant's life. If one parent consistently withdraws, while the partner distracts himself with activity, marital friction may result. In some situations one family member may be expected to remain "strong" and maintain the operational tasks in order for the family to continue functioning, but may not have time nor opportunities to grieve. The mother who is subjected to severe stress in addition to loss of a child is likely to experience a severe or abnormal grief reaction, and if lacking supportive relationships is likely to experience major difficulties.

A formal funeral service may be an important step to acknowledge at a personal and social level that a major loss has occurred.

Gorer (1959) suggested that Western society is not good at acknowledging death and may have fewer formal rituals, religious or otherwise, to assist the process of mourning. It is of interest when visiting graveyards in the small country towns of Australia to note that the parents of the infants who died a century ago often recorded this event on a small grave with a headstone which still stands, although worn by the weather and overgrown by weeds. Perhaps, although accustomed to infant deaths from many epidemics and causes, the parents of the previous centuries were better than we are at leaving a memorial of these sad occasions. I close by drawing attention to an occasion fifty years ago, when an infant death in a poor area of Liverpool was celebrated with a formal laying-out ceremony. Neighbours and friends were invited to come and see the corpse. A small urchin gleefully urged the school teacher to "come and see the dead baby, Maam, she looks so beautiful, all laid out in lace." Perhaps we are able to learn a little from this incident, that the open acknowledgement of death can be beneficial to the initiation and completion of mourning. The rites of passage which are an integral part of established cultures throughout the world developed with an important psychocultural purpose, namely, to promote adaptation in a community when faced with the inevitable changes of human existence.

CHAPTER 12

MALADAPTIVE GRIEVING
AND PATHOLOGICAL SYNDROMES

I tell you, hopeless grief is passionless

Sonnet: Grief
Elizabeth Barrett Browing

Grief following a bereavement is a universal phenomenon experienced by most individuals on several occasions during a lifetime. Vachon (1976) estimated that 10 percent of adult Canadian women are widowed at any one time and the ratio of widows to widowers is four to one. We are thus concerned with a common phenomenon. Grief has a wide range of manifestations, and a variable course. The manifestations of grief occur in the physiological, emotional, cognitive, behavioral, and social spheres, with widespread individual variation.

Clinicians and researchers have attempted to describe the core components of grief, map their progress and define a "normal" range, but there is limited agreement on this and also on what constitutes an abnormal reaction. The terminology differs and abnormal grief has been referred to as pathological, atypical, complicated, abnormal, neurotic, or unresolved. These terms are not entirely satisfactory but may be attempting to highlight different facets of grief. Grief may be viewed as pathological, in that it has a pathology, morbid, in that both physical and psychological morbility have been described, neurotic, in that defence mechanisms such as denial or idealisation are employed, unresolved, in that memories and some degree of dysphoria often persist for long periods of time, atypical, in that we are all individuals with our own unique experience and mode of expression, or complicated (life is complicated). However, the above terms attempt to draw attention to grief which has become seriously maladaptive as a result of its intensity, duration, or conflict with the expectations of society.

DEFINING ABNORMALITIES OF GRIEVING

Terminology and definitions applied to abnormalities of grieving have not always been adequately clarified. The DSM III R (1987) states that a normal bereavement reaction precludes a diagnosis of certain mood disorders and adjustment disorders, but does not describe a normal bereavement reaction. Abnormalities of grieving are not categorised as such in the DSM III R, but would presumably be largely subsumed under the categories of disorders of adjustment, mood, or anxiety, with some individuals having excessive dependent or obsessional personality traits, which may influence the course of grieving. After a particularly violent or traumatic death, the bereaved may develop a posttraumatic stress disorder, with intrusive memories, alternating with numbing, and vivid nightmares of the event.

Zisook (1987) regarded unresolved grief as a somewhat overly simplistic concept, as most, if not all people never totally resolve their grief and may experience it for years without other abnormalities. For some individuals, identification syndromes occur, with feelings of the presence of the deceased and daily visions, while others feel pain, anger, and guilt. It is open to debate at what point and to what degree these behaviors and symptoms should be a cause for concern.

An absence of grief, prolonged grief, or extreme expressions of grief, often associated with an impairment in functioning, may all become the focus of concern for other family members or health workers.

Lindemann (1944) was one of the first workers to attempt to systematically study grief reactions, following a large nightclub fire. He described a pattern of delayed grief and a pattern of distorted grief, in which there could be persistent compulsive overactivity without a sense of loss, identification with the deceased and acquisition of symptoms of the last illness of the deceased, a deterioration in health with the development of medical illness, social isolation, withdrawal and alienation and significant depression.

Volkan (1970) regarded the reactions to loss by death as being distributed along a spectrum, with pathological grief reactions occupying the middle portion of the spectrum between those of "normal" grief at one end and those who suffer from full blown neurosis or psychosomatic symptoms at the other end. The chief characteristics of pathological grief were considered to be the presence of a transitional "linking" object, chronicity of normal grief symptoms, repetitive dreams in which the deceased is alive and an inability to "bury" the lost one.

Lieberman (1978) described "morbid grief" as those processes which become blocked, leading to abnormal behavior, distorted interpersonal relationships, and physical or mental illness. He incorporated thirteen indicators of morbid grief into a scale, covering areas of avoidance, delayed reaction, the absence of expected grief, and prolonged grief. Three patterns of morbid grief were noted, including those of phobic avoidance, total absence of grieving after the death of someone close, but associated with angry feelings about the deceased and the circumstances surrounding the death, and a pattern of prolonged grief. This latter pattern often included recurrent nightmares and also the physical illnesses which are exacerbated by chronic emotional stress.

Horowitz et al. (1980) defined "pathological grief" as the intensification of grief to the level where the person is overwhelmed, resorts to maladaptive behavior, or remains interminably in the state of grief without the progression of the mourning process towards completion. It was suggested that for some people, mourning the loss of a loved one involved a process so unbearably painful, protracted or tenaciously blocked that it can be described as pathological grief. "Pathological mourning" was thought to involve processes that did not move progressively towards assimilation or accommodation but, instead, lead to stereotyped repetitions or extensive interruptions of healing.

Worden (1982) categorised complicated grief reactions into chronic, delayed, exaggerated, and masked reactions. The chronic grief reaction is prolonged and never comes to a satisfactory conclusion. This may be the commonest form of grief which presents to psychiatrists.

The delayed reaction, also known as an inhibited, suppressed, or postponed grief reaction, involves an emotional reaction at the time of the loss which is not sufficient to that loss, but on a subsequent occasion of loss, the intensity of grief is excessive. This may arise in a situation in which, following the initial bereavement, there was inadequate opportunity to grieve as a result of excessive responsibility, or a lack of social sanction for grieving.

The exaggerated reactions include excessive anxiety, phobias about death (thanatophobia), depressive feelings, or hopelessness which have become irrational or disproportionate.

Masked grief reactions are those in which individuals do not allow themselves to experience grief directly but develop a physical symptom or maladaptive behavior instead. Acting out behavior may develop after a bereavement in some adolescents who are escaping from feelings of sadness. "Alexithymia," described by Sifneos (1973), refers to the inability of some individuals to describe their feelings appropriately which may be associated with a propensity to develop somatic illnesses. Alexithymic patients may present with a masked grief reaction. Assisting the alexithymic patient to make contact with feelings of grief is a difficult therapeutic task.

Fisch (1989) described a case of a fifty-year-old woman who had experienced Holocaust terrors forty years previously and subsequently, after a bereavement, presented with a masked depression with somatic symptoms which were related to her alexithymic characteristics.

Parkes and Weiss (1983) suggested a category of "conflicted grief" which resembled delayed grief in which the relative absence of overt grief in the early postbereavement period was followed by a state of generalised anxiety, self doubt, remorse, and distress.

The definitions of abnormalities of grieving often include theoretical parameters which are derived from psychodynamic, behavioral or other models, which make a direct comparison difficult.

GRIEF AS A DISEASE

Engel (1961) has discussed the concept of grief as a disease, with a characteristic symptom profile, course, and complications. However, it could be argued that it is no more a disease than is pregnancy, which also has characteristic symptoms and recognised complications. Grief could be viewed as the response to the "lesion" of a bereavement, in which a psychological "wound" has been inflicted on the bereaved. In that situation grief could be likened to the healing response which takes place around a wound.

GRIEF, RESOLUTION, AND HOMEOSTASIS

While bereavement places an individual at risk, in that he is more isolated socially and is also disrupted as a psychobiological organism, the grief process itself could be viewed as potentially reparative. During the phase of numbness, the individual is adopting strategies of personal conservation of psychological and physical resources. Following a phase of searching and questioning, the finality of the loss sinks in, enabling subsequent restructuring of cognitive schemata and concomitant emotions so that there is a return to the status quo. The signals emitted during grieving (both vocalisations and bodily postures of withdrawal) may initially attract help and result in a socially sanctioned temporary respite from duties, which is advantageous to survival, although, if prolonged unduly, may drive away potential sources of social support.

The grief process could be regarded as a homeostatic mechanism (or series of mechanisms) which enlists social support, protects the biological integrity of the organism as well as enabling continued adaptive ego functioning and enables a realignment of physiological, cognitive, and emotional vectors to take place. As with many homeostatic mechanisms there may be a series of oscillations of the regulator or regulated factors. Hence, the alternation in the grieving person between intrusive thoughts and numbness, or between fond yearning and resentment, or between searching behavior and withdrawal. Such emotions or behaviors oscillate, with the oscillations gradually becoming smaller and often more prolonged and eventually being extinguished, so that after months or years there may, for example, only be occasional yearning which is triggered by environmental or internal cues or by deliberate active recall. The feedback loops would probably involve social relationships, intrapsychic processes, cognitive self-appraisals, and the hypothalamic-pituitary-adrenal axis, among other systems. It could be seen that a regulating factor, such as social attention or socially sanctioned withdrawal from daily activities, could result in a prolonged or abnormal grief process, while other regulators in the system, if inadequately "set," could also result in an apparent abnormality of the grieving process. Grieving which is prolonged, excessive or maladaptive could be seen to result from abnormalities in a homeostatic process of this sort.

RISK FACTORS IN
THE DEVELOPMENT OF ABNORMAL GRIEF

Parkes (1980) characterised the high-risk bereaved woman as being a young widow with children living at home, with no close relatives living nearby, who was a timid, clinging person who has reacted badly to separation in the past, and who had a previous history of depressive illness. In addition, an overreliant or ambivalent relationship with her husband, an unexpected or untimely death, an inhibition of the expression of emotion as a result of cultural or familial factors and, other concomitant stress would all increase the likelihood of an adverse reaction.

Other workers have also examined these features. Raphael (1977) identified a perceived lack of social support, an ambivalent relationship with the deceased, and concurrent life events as risk factors for developing abnormal bereavement reactions.

Greenblatt (1978) listed factors which could delay or suppress grief, including social stigma around the loss (which could occur today following a death from A.I.D.S.); uncertainty about whether the loss had occurred (which may occur following a military action); the presence of old, unresolved losses; the presence of multiple past losses; an overcrowded or unappealing cemetery; and concern about the health and welfare of young children which may inhibit the full expression of feelings.

Bowlby (1980) suggested that those prone to disordered mourning tended either to make affectional relationships marked by anxiety and ambivalence, or to be compulsive caregivers, or to claim independence of all affectional ties, which could be termed "pseudo-independence."

Stroebe et al. (1983) considered that men who lose their wives are at a higher risk than women who lose their husbands.

Alarcon (1984) hypothesised that complicated bereavement is primarily a reflection of personality disorder, if a major affective disorder is absent.

Parkes (1985) postulated a grief-prone personality who tends to react strongly to separations.

Jacobsen (1986) described a case of a fifty-six-year-old man whose pathological grief reaction of twenty-five years duration arose in the setting of an impoverished childhood, social withdrawal, an avoidant personality, and multiple subsequent losses. The theory of Horowitz et al. (1980) (which attributes the origin of abnormal grief to the intensification of normal grief processes as a result of the reemergence of latent self-images and role relationship models that had been held in check by a positive relationship with the deceased) was used to understand the intensity of grief in this case.

Rynearson (1987) discussed abnormal grief reactions which arise following an unnatural death from homicide, suicide, or accident, which may give rise to existential dilemmas or dichotomies that are inherently unresolvable in the mind of the bereaved. The compulsive inquiry by the bereaved to establish the locus of responsibility, the purpose of the death or if it was intended, often remains unanswered.

Stroebe et al. (1987) have elaborated on the lack of social support in placing the bereaved individual significantly at risk.

The complete absence of a grief reaction may occur in the affectionless psychopath in whom close attachment bonds do not arise and who may also experience sadistic pleasure in observing death or killing. A highly disturbed, sadistic murderer who was recently imprisoned in Sydney claimed that he loved to see his victims staggering around wounded and that he would kill his mother if there was no one else around to kill.

However, a less intense grief reaction occurs in individuals whose attachment bonds are not so great, who may possess some schizoid personality traits. A very intense rage reaction, sometimes accompanied by self-destructive behavior, occurs in the bereaved individual with borderline personality traits.

The individual who possesses psychological resilience, which is demonstrated by an ability to cope with stress in an adaptive way, who has experienced a secure relationship of attachment in childhood, and who has maintained a family or social network on which he can rely is likely to cope well with bereavement. In such an individual, the experience of a bereavement and successful working through of grief on one occasion may facilitate the working through of subsequent grief reactions. Although painful feelings are still evoked, the individual in this situation knows what to expect and may have learned some techniques for coping with grief.

However, the individual who has coped poorly with bereavement previously or who has experienced unresolved losses, may, on the occasion of a subsequent bereavement, experience similar difficulties and also reexperience the previously "unfinished grief."

OTHER ABNORMALITIES OF GRIEVING

It is generally accepted that many of the symptoms following a bereavement resemble those or are sometimes identical to those found in a depressive disorder. A psychiatric disorder of a different type sometimes occurs after a bereavement.

There is some evidence to suggest that the stress of loss or bereavement may precipitate a manic episode. Ambelas (1979) screened the case notes of sixty-seven manic patients for independent life events over a four-week period prior to admission and compared them with a control group of surgical admissions. Four times as many manic patients had an independent life event closely preceding admission, while fourteen manic patients experienced a loss or threatened loss and, of these, five experienced a bereavement. Rosenman et al. (1986) described a case of mania following bereavement, which prompted correspondence in the *British Journal of Psychiatry* indicating other such patients. However, it may be pointed out that in the case described by Rosenman a biological vulnerability to affective disorder was already present and that bereavement was acting as a nonspecific stress. Mcloughlin et al. (1987) described a case of affective psychosis in a mentally handicapped woman. I described a young man who developed a manic episode after the death of a girlfriend (Haig, 1988).

Hickie et al. (1989) described the development of a panic disorder in a husband and wife and a school phobia in a son soon after the death of the father of the husband from leukemia.

A bizarre response following bereavement was described by Gardner et al. (1977). Six cases were reported in which the bereaved kept the deceased's body for periods ranging from one week to ten years. Three of the cases were Orthodox Jews, who would normally follow a clearly defined mourning ritual and burial within twenty-four hours, but failed to initiate this. Two of the individuals were psychotic.

Pathological grieving may occur after a spontaneous abortion, but not be acknowledged as such unless recognised by the therapist (see Corney et al., 1974).

The death of a closely loved pet may be followed by a pathological grief reaction. Keddie (1977) described three women who developed pathological grief reactions after the death of dogs which had been pets for thirteen years. These reactions were resolved by psychiatric treatment.

Snowdon et al. (1978) discussed "feigned bereavement" in twelve cases, which appeared to be a form of abnormal illness behavior or Munchausen's syndrome. Most of the patients appeared to be depressed on admission to hospital, often used more than one name, had been admitted to hospital on many previous occasions and appeared to be seeking sympathy or attention.

A posttraumatic stress disorder may follow a particularly traumatic or horrifying death, in which the bereaved has vivid and frightening recollections of the event, heightened anxiety, and nightmares.

Warnes (1985) hypothesised that a state of "frozen" grief and inability to mourn created a secondary type of alexithymia which was described in three cases, who were helped by understanding nonverbal communications and bodily and dream phenomena.

CONCLUSIONS

A common consensus on what constitutes a normal grief reaction would assist in arriving at a definition of abnormal grief. While a total absence of grief would usually be regarded as abnormal, individuals demonstrate a wide variation in their response to loss. When grief is prolonged at a high level, is unbearably distressing, or is becoming maladaptive to the daily functioning of that person, the abnormality comes to the attention of health personnel, who attempt to describe the problem, understand it on the basis of a particular theory, and then treat it.

The possibility that grief itself is part of the healing process or that grief is part of a homeostatic system with feedback loops and regulators, which are psychological, social, and biological in origin, is discussed.

The risk factors which have been described by different workers emphasise the circumstances of the loss, the nature of the relationship in terms of dependence, ambivalence and attachment, and the level of social support. The personality of the bereaved also appears to play an important part in the pattern of grieving, and would also effect the nature of the relationship with the deceased both pre and postbereavement.

The ability of bereavement, as a major loss, and stressor to precipitate specific psychiatric disorders has been discussed. It is probable that bereavement acts as a nonspecific stressor which precipitates or "brings forward" in time the occurrence of some disorders, but may also act as a specific precipitant of mood disorders which have a symptom profile remarkably like that of grief itself. For some individuals anxiety is their characteristic psychophysiological response to threats of loss or to loss itself, and they will respond accordingly following a bereavement.

Chapter 13

THE MANAGEMENT OF GRIEF

Can I see another's grief
And not seek for kind relief?

On Another's Sorrow
William Blake

It may be an indictment on our modern structure of society that there is a perceived need for grief counselors. Previous eras and more primitive societies may have provided opportunities for grieving as an integral part of the social fabric. Death was much more familiar and immediate, often taking place in the home with the circle of family and friends looking on, so there was no denying its existence. Elias (1985) discussed this and the contrasting modern isolation of the dying person in a hospital or hospice, well cared for physically, the bodily organs being well preserved by medical experts, but living in loneliness with a group of complete strangers with whom he has had no previous contact in his life. The potential loneliness of this death, hygienic maybe, but sterile in an interactional sense with the family and friends, could lead to corresponding feelings of isolation and noninvolvement and guilt by the family and friends who are kept at arm's length. At the same time, there has been a decline in the use of traditional mourning rituals and religious supports discussed by Gorer (1965) which may also predispose to an increase in abnormal or delayed grief reactions. Our modern societies have, through these two developments, namely, the removal of dying from the home, with its social support network, and the decline of traditional mourning practices, thereby interfered with the processes of grieving. We are still in the process of tackling the joint problems of how to reduce the loneliness of the dying and how to enable relatives and friends to grieve in a meaningful way.

A study of more than one hundred people who were bereaved in the United Kingdom, conducted by Wright et al. (1988), revealed that many people felt distressed by the way in which the death of their relative was broken to them, communication with hospital staff was poor and bereavement counseling was rarely offered in the health services. The attitude of hospital staff was often found to be impersonal and cold. Individuals were very distressed if they were not with a relative at the time of death. Some were not summoned in time, some were refused permission to stay and some were made to feel in the way. Relatives of the deceased felt at their most vulnerable immediately after death, some requiring privacy in which to grieve with their family, some requiring a need to talk, which was not responded to, and some requiring practical guidance about postdeath procedures. Relatives reported that they found the controlled professionalism of some staff (presumably a protective mechanism on the part of the staff) to be intolerable, whereas when staff showed that they, too, were touched by the death, this was regarded as a sign of shared humanity and was comforting. The study highlighted the need for appropriate services in the U.K. health services for the large number of bereaved relatives.

From the above report it would seem that staff at many points in health services require an awareness as to the needs of bereaved relatives. A practical account of how staff in an emergency department (which is often an important initial point of contact with the bereaved) should approach relatives is given by Dubin et al, (1986). They suggested that an understanding of the dynamics of grief is important, as is familiarity with the range of responses following bereavement, including histrionic, stoical, shocked, disbelieving, and the angry responses. It was not thought appropriate to inform the next of kin of a sudden death over the telephone. Rather he or she should be summoned to come to the hospital immediately as a serious illness or injury had occurred in their relative, and they should be informed about the death on arrival in the hospital.

The staff should comfort by touching or holding the survivor, if appropriate and should be aware of (and tolerate) an angry outburst by the bereaved or may need to listen patiently to an obsessional review of events. The staff may be subjected to demands for proof of the identity of the deceased. Guilty comments by the survivor should be discouraged. The viewing of the body may be of great importance. If the body is mutilated, the family should be informed in advance. Blood and emesis should be removed prior to viewing by the family. Arrangements should be made for a family member or friend to remain with the survivor for the next twenty-four to forty-eight hours. All the above recommendations would appear to be soundly based on considerations of the dynamics of grief. Unexpected or untimely death is more likely to be followed by more severe or abnormal grief reactions (see Chapter 12). Some of these grief reactions could be mitigated by sensitive handling by hospital personnel in the emergency department. Unfortunately there is sometimes a tendency for staff, who are working in these areas, which are stressful and often busy, to distance themselves emotionally from the patients and relatives. Nevertheless they may play a crucial role with respect to the subsequent development of a normal or pathological grief reaction in the relatives, so it is important for them to attempt to acquire some of the basic skills in handling the relatives in a humane and therapeutic way.

A particularly difficult situation for the emergency department to deal with emotionally is that of the patient who has taken an overdose, sometimes as a suicidal gesture or sometimes in the course of an addictive habit, or who has made some other form of self-destructive gesture, and dies in the emergency room. The staff may perceive the patient as a despicable piece of humanity who has had the affrontery to waste the valuable time and resources of the emergency department and has increased the hospital mortality statistics. The reception which the relatives are likely to experience from staff in the above scenario is hardly likely to be welcoming. Suicide is often a difficult situation to come to terms with, as it induces feelings of great fear, rage, guilt, and relentless depression in relatives and is stigmatised by society (Lukas et al., 1988). An initial cold rejection by staff in the emergency department could exacerbate the relatives' feelings of rejection and guilt and pave the way for a pathological grief reaction with increased morbidity. The principles of care suggested by Dubin (1986) should be equally applicable to the management of the relative of the suicide, with recognition that the relative himself may represent an increased suicide risk immediately. Few staff in hospitals may have time for or be attuned to the needs of the bereaved. The report by Wright et al. (1988) drew attention to the very small number of "bereavement officers" in hospitals in the U.K. who could advise other staff on handling bereavement issues.

Many of the aspects of bereavement are dealt with serendipitously by different agencies and health professionals. Greaving individuals or families may be helped in many different milieux, including health, educational, church, workplace, and social settings. The family itself is a potentially good forum for therapeutic grieving. The grief counselor should utilise these resources appropriately.

PRACTICES WHICH FACILITATE NORMAL GRIEVING

There are episodes around the time of death in which the processes of grieving may be initiated and promoted. The following account contains suggestions regarding practices which are facilitative and could be applied in many different cultural settings.

1. Anticipatory Grief

If possible, a stage of anticipatory grief may assist the bereaved subsequently. Relatives may require help initially with the clarification of the diagnosis and prognosis and their acceptance, and subsequently support. Meares (1981), using a letter written by John Keats during his terminal illness as an example, indicated the value of "saying good-bye" before death at a time following the Kübler-Ross stage of acceptance of death, but preceding the stage of detachment. At this time the dying person begins to view his coming death through the eyes of the survivors, lets them know that they have been loved and valued, and so leaves the world in peace. It is also possible for the parent who has previously devalued or rejected a child as a result of his own negative projections to release the survivor from the spell of his own pathology before he finally dies. During anticipatory grieving both parties may undergo some grieving for losses which are already occurring, and may, to a limited extent, prepare themselves for the forthcoming departure. Unfinished emotional business may be finally tackled. It may be possible to plan tentatively for the future without the partner.

2. Supporting the Dying Person

It may be important for a relative to feel that they have done everything possible to look after the dying person and to minimise his discomfort. It may be reassuring for the dying person to be nursed at home, provided this is practical and the relationship with the relative has generally been a good one. While verbal communication may be limited towards the end, the dying person may be comforted by the presence of a close relative, and nonverbal contact may be of great value. The likelihood of excessive guilt is diminished by the application of this principle.

3. Postdeath Procedures

Attention has already been drawn to the importance of the communications and approaches by staff in the emergency room in the situation of sudden death. The manner in which the news of death is communicated to the bereaved relative can never soften the blow completely, but can be given in a considerate and compassionate way. It is important not to leave a close relative alone in the immediate period of bereavement. The initial news of death may appear to be ignored or not believed. The viewing of the body is regarded as important by many authorities on grief counseling. It may only be that the realisation of death occurs after viewing the body, and this realisation may require reinforcement before the inevitability of death finally sinks in. Pathological grief may develop if the body is not viewed. The community nurse, family physician, priest, or funeral director may all become involved with the initial stages of grief management and become defacto grief counselors. In the state of numbness which is common in the bereaved initially, practical help with funeral arrangements and the questions about autopsy and immediate living arrangements may be required. If the bereaved spouse is expected to take responsibility for all of these aspects prematurely, she may have insufficient time or energy to initiate grieving, and may switch from a state of numbness to a state of pseudo-independence and apparent coping, only to develop a pathological reaction later.

4. Participation in Funeral Ceremonies

An opportunity to participate in a culturally acceptable funeral is of importance to both bereaved adults and children. Most funeral ceremonies reinforce the fact that a particular individual has died and is no longer functioning as a member of the living community. The deceased is named, referred to in personal terms, talked about or prayed for while in the presence of the coffin with the body inside. Individuals who have missed the funeral may complain that it took a long time to begin grieving properly, feel guilty or incomplete. Mothers of sons killed in action in which the body is never recovered have a common problem in accepting that their son is dead initially and may grieve for years or even a lifetime. Memorial services to battalions which have been wiped out or unmarked graves can never replace the personal funeral service for an individual. The opportunity to see others expressing emotion in a socially supportive setting may be a useful cue to initiate grieving.

Children may find funeral ceremonies beneficial, even though they do not fully understand all of the proceedings. They are able to learn that adults experience strong emotions and that it is acceptable to express them, and they appreciate that it is a very special, albeit sad occasion, to honor the deceased. They also feel that they share in the occasion as part of a family.

For the individual who has been brought up in a particular religion, it may be very comforting to know that the deceased is now being taken care of in the customary manner. Sympathetic and appropriate support from a religious leader and members of the congregation may also be valued.

5. Continuing Recognition by Society of the Grieving Process

In some cultures, other rituals and ceremonies are conducted following the funeral ceremony, sometimes up to a year or more afterwards, thus giving recognition to the timespan of grief. During the initial stages there may be a socially sanctioned withdrawal of the closely bereaved from their normal duties and social engagements. The widower or widow is not expected to go to work, or is fed or looked after by close relatives. In many modern industrial societies, these needs are not fully recognised, and only a few days "compassionate" leave from work may be permitted. In the postindustrial era, where it is no longer necessary to have a large pool of workers attending to repetitive manual or clerical jobs for many hours every day, there may be more time available for attending to personal grief or the grief of others.

6. An End to Mourning

At some stage it may be necessary for society to remind the bereaved individual that the deceased should be left in peace, and normal activities may be resumed. However, it is customary in some societies for widows to wear black for the rest of their lives and this may trap them into a state of perpetual mourning. However, the subjective experience of grief in these widows may not correspond to a state of deep mourning. Black may even be used to good effect by some widows to appear very avant garde and fashionable.

In all of the above practices, permission to express emotions, some opportunity to share the internal experiences with others, support from the social network, and recognition of the distress of the individual are all important ingredients for the promotion of normal grieving.

The practices as described constitute a framework which is culturally and individually congruent and also occur over a time scale which is compatible with the intrinsic biological time scale of most human grief reactions.

Grief counselors should be aware that if an individual is already involved in a cultural framework of grief such as the one described, it is good counsel to help to support that individual in that framework. It only becomes necessary to help to create a new framework if the individual has been alienated from a framework or requests help with his grieving because he has no framework. With the alienation of increasing numbers of people in society and the abandonment of traditional forms of mourning, the grief counselor's expertise may be called on more frequently.

Chapter 14

GRIEF COUNSELING:
THE ART OF ENABLING TRANSITION

THE ASSESSMENT OF GRIEF

The grief counselor accumulates much data on the grieving patient who is at risk and has been referred or self-referred. If there is a referral agent it is of importance to collect date from that source. Background information on the client and the concerns of the referring agent are both relevant for the counseling process. Initial details about the death, the relationship with the deceased, and the emotions and conflicts engendered by the death need to be obtained. Historical details regarding other important relationships of the bereaved person, his personality, life style, previous level of functioning, previous major losses, and concurrent stressors need to be established in order to determine the optimal intervention. Losses in childhood, particularly of parents, may be relevant if they have not been adequately integrated. A current loss may reactivate memories and conflicts engendered by an early loss. It is relevant to know whether culturally compatible mourning ceremonies have taken place and whether the bereaved person was able to participate. An appraisal of the emotions currently experienced by the client, such as sadness, anxiety, guilt, or anger, is also made.

However, some flexibility of approach by the counselor is of importance in accumulating the above details. The client should intially be given an opportunity to express himself spontaneously at his own speed without undue prompting from the counselor. If there are then major gaps in data the counselor may express an interest in knowing more about these areas. The counselor may at times need to tolerate silences which may be painful and should not be rushing to fill these with a clamor for detail or advice which may be premature. Raphael (1983) refers to a "therapeutic assessment of the bereaved," which suggests that the provision of some details may be therapeutic and further the understanding and acceptance of the client.

123

An individual who has never freely expressed emotions may be reluctant to commence this in grief counseling. However, the opportunity to review the events which have taken place and the problems which have emerged may be valued. This may then lead into a discussion about feelings and attitudes about the deceased, and if supported in this the client may feel safe to express feelings more openly. The issue of the catharsis of emotions versus their control is of importance in formulating an individual treatment plan.

Friends of the bereaved individual may need to understand that their toleration and support is required for a substantial period of time. There is a misconception by some relatives that grieving should only last for a few weeks and they may give inappropriate advice to "snap out of it" or "pull yourself together," followed by pressure to seek medical help for what may be a normal grief reaction. Provided there is no major underlying pathology the best intervention from the doctor may be to give permission for a continuation of grieving, which is normal, but with help from family, friends or some other social support group. Widow-to-widow counseling programs may be useful.

The grieving person may require relief from work responsibilities for a time. The ability to focus energy on new projects may be limited, as the grieving individual is, in a Freudian sense, devoting his or her energy to the task of mourning. Premature advice from well intentioned (or impatient) friends or relatives to move house, find another companion, or throw away the wife's or husband's clothing may interfere with the grieving processes. The bereaved person requires time in which to consider and then to finalise these decisions, and the grief counselor may need to emphasise this. The assessment of the client often involves obtaining information on many aspects of his life in order to fully understand the emotional meaning of the loss for that individual in addition to the social and economic implications.

The family structure may modify the course of grief. Paul (1967) hypothesised that there was a direct relationship between the maladaptive response to the death of a loved person and the fixity of symbiotic relationships within the family. Clinical experience confirms the difficulty which rigid families have in adopting to the death of a key member. Overrigid families may even have difficulty in acknowledging that death has occurred.

The counselor should be familiar with both the verbal and nonverbal communications of the client. Observations of facial expressions, bodily posture, tone of voice, and the reluctance or willingness to become engaged in the session all provide clues to the underlying emotional processes. The spontaneity and congruence of the emotions, particularly when the deceased is being discussed, are indicative of the progress of grieving. During an initial assessment, the counselor is already attempting to convey empathic understanding to the client.

THE ASSESSMENT OF COMPLICATED GRIEF

If the grieving process has become unduly prolonged, excessive, or bizarre or additional severe pathology is emeging, the grief counselor should reassess the situation and if necessary seek additional advice from other professionals. If physical complaints are prominent, such as breathlessness, chest pain, or prolonged fatigue, the advice of a medical practitioner should be obtained without delay. Physical morbidity may be increased in bereaved individuals, whether as a result of self-neglect, increased use of tobacco or alcohol, deficient diet, or as a result of stress-induced changes mediated though the endocrine and autoimmune systems. A thorough physical evaluation of the client may be conducted by a medical practitioner and any necessary investigations organised.

Where psychological symptoms are prominent and persistent, evaluation by a psychiatrist may be advisable. Many psychiatrists have expertise in the management of complicated grief reactions. A psychiatric disorder, often with depressive features, may emerge following bereavement. The symptoms of grief are often similar to those of a depressive disorder, with complaints of feelings of depression, poor appetite, weight loss, and insomnia. If the complaints of depressed feelings are severe, unremitting, and persist or if there is a morbid preoccupation with worthlessness, prolonged social incapacity, marked psychomotor retardation, or expressions of suicidal intent, it is likely that a major depression is developing which requires treatment.

The bereaved individual who becomes euphoric or very irritable, and appears to be insensitive to the recent severe loss may be developing a hypomanic episode. This may be accompanied by increased talkativeness, a flight of ideas, grandiose ideas, participation in unrestrained buying sprees or foolish business investments.

An increased use of drugs where there has been a previous habit is not uncommon, so that the detrimental effects of alcohol or central nervous system depressants may become prominent, with resulting difficulties in concentration and mood changes, or major symptoms of intoxication or withdrawal.

Anxiety symptoms may predominate following a bereavement and become a cause for concern. Symptoms of a panic disorder include a sudden onset of fear, which may be accompanied by shortness of breath, dizziness, faintness, choking, palpitations, acceleration of pulse, trembling, sweating, nausea, depersonalisation, numbness, chest pains, fear of dying, or a fear of going crazy. An individual who has a previous history of chronic agoraphobia may experience particular difficulties when a spouse on whom they have been very dependent dies as they may be confronted with the need to leave the security of their home which may precipitate anxiety symptoms.

The ageing bereaved individual may have become increasingly dependent on his or her spouse as a result of a decline in functional capacity consistent with the changes of ageing. Following the bereavement, some of the difficulties in coping or reestablishing social contacts may take longer to overcome than in the younger person. An early dementing process may sometimes come to attention for the first time following a bereavement, especially if their deficiences were compensated for by the spouse prior to that time. Assessment in this situation requires psychiatric expertise as there may be a range of underlying organic pathologies, in addition to complex social and psychological factors. Some symptoms which superficially resemble those of an early dementia may be symptomatic of a depressive disorder which will respond to antidepressant treatments.

A careful history of previous psychiatric disorder and a familial history of such disorder provide additional data which assist in arriving at a more informed psychiatric diagnosis. When a psychiatric disorder appears to be emerging, the counselor should not hesitate to seek psychiatric advice.

Confirmation of changes in the mental state and social functioning may be reported by relatives or friends. If grieving appears to be very problematic it may be helpful to interview a relative or individual who has known the bereaved person for some years to confirm details of previous personality, social relationships, and coping skills.

An unresolved grief reaction may not present directly to a doctor but be manifested indirectly by a physical symptom, which on inquiry appears to be identical to a symptom experienced by a relative who died with whom there has been a strong unconscious identification.

Other clues to unresolved grief have been described by Lazare (1979) and include an intensification of fresh grief whenever the deceased is mentioned, a relatively minor event triggering off an intense grief reaction, themes of loss emerging repeatedly in the clinical interview, the unwillingness of the bereaved to move material possessions belonging to the deceased, the making of radical changes in life style following a death, the long history of a subclinical depression, a compulsion to imitate the dead person, self-destructive impulses, unaccountable sadness occurring at a certain time each year, a phobia about illness or death, and avoidance behavior concerning the grave or funeral ritual.

However, selecting one of the above "clues" to unresolved grief could be misleading if taken in isolation, as many individuals would feel sad or reexperience grief when reviewing certain aspects of their life and others would be forced to make major changes in their living arrangements following a bereavement. Certain of the other "clues" could be a manifestation of varibles other than unresolved grief. A long history of a subclinical depression or self-destructive impulses could result from a genetic disposition to a mood disorder, while sadness occurring at certain times each year could result from a seasonal affective disorder, which may be related to the duration of daylight.

FACILITATING THE PROGRESS OF GRIEF

The counselor who demonstrates concern for the client is providing an important basis for the subsequent working through of problems. The framework provided by the counselor himself may consist of the opportunity to spend a number of sessions with that counselor, during which time the bereaved client has the opportunity to talk about the deceased, the circumstances of the loss, and any other pressing matters which are relevant to the client together with the opportunity to share emotions which arise from the loss with the counselor. This latter process appears to be the key to the successful working through of many grief reactions.

The venue for grief counseling may be an office or the individual's home. An office may feel safer for the individual who has experienced a traumatic death at home, but the home may provide more reminders of the deceased and be useful to initiate or promote grieving.

In the initial stages of grieving it may be comforting for the very distressed bereaved person who is having difficulty verbalising (or hearing anything spoken) to be touched or physically held. Raphael (1983) drew attention to the importance of touch in comforting the acutely bereaved, but pointed out that this may not sit well with other therapeutic frameworks. It is doubtful whether it would be helpful for the professional grief counselor to have much physical contact with the client at a later stage of grief counseling and, if this occurs extensively, supervision of the counselor may be appropriate. A comforting hand on the knee may not be perceived as such by all grieving widows.

The chief task of grief counseling, which should be promoted within the developing counselor-client relationship is the facilitation of an adaptive grief reaction. The client is helped to accept the reality of the death, although possibly painful. He is given the opportunity to express affects of sadness, pain, anger, guilt, fear, or relief. He is encouraged to integrate these affects and eventually to modulate or neutralise the most extreme in order to facilitate an emotional withdrawal from the deceased. He is encouraged, after an appropriate time, to cope with the realities of his everyday life and eventually to become more actively involved in family and social relationships again. The counselor should not have a preconceived notion of how an individual must grieve, but should be aware of the range of possibilities for grieving in that individual and the need for the client to undergo a journey, even if the route may appear circuitous. The counselor may at times be travelling with the client, at times may lag behind the client, and at times may be indicating a direction to the client.

The affects of sadness, a sense of loss and painful yearning for the deceased, which has a repetitive quality, may be an important part of many grief reactions. The client (and counselor) may need to learn to experience and tolerate these affects before they diminish. A premature attempt to escape from these affects may be made by clients who resort to alcohol or other drugs. A decision to sell a house or relocate in another city may also be an attempt to flee from such feelings. The ability to cry and share some of these feelings may greatly assist the bereaved. Guilt also arises not uncommonly in Western societies. The regrets that not enough had been done for the deceased or angry words had been exchanged prior to the death are not unexpected. However, when guilt develops a self castigating property and becomes extreme there may be underlying feelings of unexpressed anger towards the deceased. The counselor himself may feel "beaten about the head" by the client who is "going on a guilt trip" Guilt should be gently discouraged if it is clearly unjustified and a realistic cognitive reappraisal of the circumstances around which the guilt is focussed many need to be performed on several occasions before the guilt is diminished.

Anxiety may be manifested in somatic symptoms, in which a racing heart, light-headedness, and sweating occur, but is usually accompanied by a feeling of tension or fear. This may be a nonspecific response to separation from an attachment figure, but may have a specific focus in that the bereaved individual is fearful of living alone, facing new or different responsibilities, or has an existential anxiety of personal death or annihilation. The presence of an understanding counselor may reduce the anxiety considerably. Review of the feared situation with the client will reassure and encourage alternate coping strategies.

The modulation of the affects of grief may sometimes be achieved by catharsis. Cognitive reappraisal may be of benefit if the affects are excessive or prolonged. A repetitive experience of an idea or image which is associated with a painful affect (which is a normal part of grieving) may result in desensitisation, in which the emotional arousal is progressively reduced. Techniques to modulate affects which rely only on suppression or diversion are usually regarded as unhelpful in the intial stages of bereavement. Avoidance strategies were not regarded as helpful in the study by Weinberg (1985). However, in the later stages of grieving, clients are likely to find that they benefit from diverting their thoughts or activities to other areas when they have decided it is reasonable.

Humor which is spontaneous may for a short time reduce the pain of grief. It is possible for an individual to acknowledge the tragedy of a situation, to gain a little emotional distance, and to convert the pain of a situation into pleasure through the utilisation of humor (see Haig, 1988). The client who utilises humor in order to cope with the pain of grief should be encouraged as this is one of the more adaptive defenses (see Vaillant, 1977). The grief counselor may in later sessions with the client resonate to the client's humor with his own humor, but should be aware that aggressive humor should not be utilised as it may be perceived as an attack. Humor may also be introduced with clients who are rigidly locked into a cycle of increasingly egocentric grieving. Humor may at times reduce demoralisation, encourage objectivity, and promote sharing, but should only be used in the service of the client by a counselor who is "in tune" with the client.

Another technique which may be utilised in later sesions is the telling of anecdotes which are about individuals who have been through the grieving process in different ways and indicate to the client different therapeutic possibilities. Stories may be of particular use in children and adolescents and serve as therapeutic metaphors with which they can identify and utilise. Occasionally a film may trigger off a reworking of grief. A film such as "The Accidental Tourist" which concerns a couple's separation following the death of their ten-year-old son, and the subsequent expression of grief by the father may be a useful focus for adults who are in similar situations. If the conflict within a story resonates with the client's conflict, the story (or film) attains the status of a metaphor, which has therapeutic implications and can be used for the benefit of the client.

Christie et al. (1987) utilised the film "The Never Ending Story" with an eleven-year-old boy whose mother had suicided and who had become blocked in his grieving. The hero of the film, whose mother had died, commenced a journey in which there was a mission to save Fantasia (the land of human hopes and dreams). On this journey the hero negotioated the Swamps of Sadness, entered the Gate of Confidence, faced himself in the Magic Mirror Gate, defeated both the Werewolf and the Nothing, before he finally helped to restore Fantasia again, after naming his dead mother out loud. The film was used as a therapeutic metaphor by the therapist, served as a model for grief, and as a framework for the therapy which was conducted.

For some individuals their grief may be dominated by anger. This may occur intensely in the person for many years who has felt let down or abandoned. The anger may be directed towards the medical professions, which may result, in an extreme situation, in death threats or, in other situations, in litigious behavior. The counselor who becomes involved should be careful to retain an objective stance while still trying to understand the point of view of the client. Communication of the counselor's understanding to the client may be very reassuring to the client, who feels understood, but may then begin to distance himself from his unmodulated emotions.

An emotionally aroused client may be inappropriately encouraged to channel his anger into a malpractice suit, which is not necessarily therapeutic, and will not bring the dead back to life and may, because of the protracted nature of the legal process, interfere with the process of grieving. Occassionally intense anger may be diverted to a socially appropriate enterprise, such as fund-raising for cancer research or hospital support services or political activities. The relatives of a murder victim may, in a process of reaction formation, reverse their anger towards the murderer and become advocates for abolition of the death penalty or prison reform.

Many bereaved people become polarised between idealisation or devaluation of the deceased and may benefit from counseling to reevaluate their positive and negative attitudes to the deceased. If there has been a hostile or passive-dependent relationship with the deceased the client may continue to experience marked affective arousal associated with repeated intrusive images of the deceased. In this situation more intensive therapy may be required.

Some clients may require reassurance that they are not crazy if they experience considerable anger or guilt initially, or if they experience a strong sense of presence of the deceased or briefly see or hear the deceased. The latter phenomena are more likely to occur in a location which was frequented by the deceased and may be a source of comfort to the bereaved, only to be followed by disappointment because the deceased is no longer alive.

A pattern of semidenial may sometimes be evident in the thinking or actions of the bereaved, with a tendency to think and behave as if the deceased were still there. An extra place may be set at the table, imaginary conversations may be conducted with the bereaved, but at the same time acknowledging that the deceased is not really alive. It is not necessary for intervention in most situations of this type. A simple review of what the bereaved is doing in relation to the deceased may help to clarify the purpose and usefulness of these behaviors. An acceptance that in the future a reunion in another life will occur may be comforting to the bereaved who maintain religious beliefs of this sort. Grieving behavior and intrusive thoughts diminish in frequency over the months. If the grieving behavior does not diminish, is causing significant distress, or is interfering with the life of the bereaved person, the counselor may consider further strategies to promote grieving.

When helping the client who is blocked in grieving the counselor may utilise techniques such as guided visual imagery, in which the client is encouraged to visualise the deceased, or the empty chair technique, in which imaginary conversations may be carried on with the deceased. Writing a letter to the deceased spouse may help a client to organise thoughts and feelings. The client may be encouraged to talk about a photograph or memento of the deceased. It is possible to reenact the funeral either in imagination or by using role playing techniques, in order to trigger grief which has been suppressed. The goal is for the client to accept and integrate the loss.

The desire of some clients may be to visualise or remember the deceased more clearly and when the indistinct memories of the deceased have been clarified, the client feels more at ease and able to resume daily activities again.

Some bereaved individuals may hunger for relationships as there is a major hiatus in their life. This is more likely to occur in those with a limited social circle or those with strong dependency needs.

The expectation that the grief counselor will fill this vacuum needs to be handled cautiously. The grief counselor may for a time act as a powerful support figure and therapeutic progress may occur because there is an attachment bond. Transference occurring in the relationship, in which previous attachments and associated feelings are transferred to the counselor, should be recognized and, if appropriate, discussed with the client several sessions before the agreed termination date. The counselor may be sorely missed. The client may need to arrange to have friends, relatives, or support figures when counseling has finished with whom he can talk if the need arises. Some of the feeling evoked by a separation or death may be stimulated by the termination of therapy. It would not be unusual for the client to have some ambivalent feelings towards the counselor at times, which may be used to mirror and lead into a discussion about feelings towards the deceased. At the end of therapy, feedback to the client about progress and realistic reassurance about the future are important. It would be unrealistic to expect the client two months after bereavement not to continue to have some manifestations of grieving. Reassurance about the normality of some grief symptoms, praise for achievements and gains, and suggestions about other contact persons or support groups are all part of the counseling process. Individuals who lack social skills or have been demoralised may require active encouragement to participate again in a more rewarding way in a family or social network. The "secondary gains" of bereavement in which individuals are initially excused from participating in routine work and social activities may need to be reduced with the help of the counselor in order for the bereaved individual to become integrated again. There is certainly a time for grieving and a time for living which may need to be reinforced by the counselor.

The concept of "dosing" grief, or limiting the hours in the day which the bereaved should focus on grief, is interesting, and suggests a possibility of self-control. Janson (1985) decribed a time limiting technique in which the client selects a time of day and an area of the home in which he feels comfortable and safe, and during this time focuses on thoughts about the deceased, utilising a life review and diary. Thoughts about the deceased which are disruptive to the daily functioning are reserved for this time.

Later in the course of grieving, individuals being to engage in rewarding activities again. On occasion these activities may be an important means of distraction from painful grief thoughts. However, frantic activity or seeking out many sexual partners may suggest that the grief has become blocked and the client may require further assistance.

The counselor who has qualities which include a warm personality, the ability to tolerate distress, with whom the client can identify (and vice versa) and who can develop an understanding of the client will facilitate progress more rapidly. Some clients may feel more comfortable initially with a counselor who has come from a similar cultural background. The more subtle linguistic nuances may sometimes only be understood in short-term counseling by a counselor from the same ethnic background. Raphael (1983) suggested that natural comforting responses may develop more easily between females. It is of interest that a plea for more understanding and help for bereaved fathers who traditionally have not been encouraged to express emotions comes from a woman, Jean Scully (1985).

The grief counselor's understanding of grief may be expanded by having experienced and worked through a personal major bereavement. However, if he is still coming to terms with a recent bereavement this may interfere with his ability to assist the client. Worden (1982) encourages trainee grief counselors to explore their own history of loses, and to participate in role playing techniques as a means of gaining more understanding of how clients may feel. An awareness of the wide range of grief reactions, with differing manifestations and different time scales is of importance to the grief counselor.

The counselor should recognise his own limitations and be aware of the need to seek supervision and, if necessary, to refer to other professionals when clients are not progressing or in whom major pathology is prominent. Also it is wise to recognise that there is a limit to the number of distressed clients who can reasonably be treated without depleting the emotional resources of the counselor. The counselor should have other professional and social activities which are not directly associated with grief counseling and help to maintain a fresh perspective and guarded optimism in work which may be demoralising or difficult.

Chapter 15

GRIEF COUNSELING:
SPECIAL CATEGORIES AND TECHNIQUES

GRIEF COUNSELING IN CHILDREN

The counselor who has contact with the bereaved child should be aware of the different concepts about death in the child, which depend on the cognitive stage of development (see Chapter 9), the patterns of grieving which differ from the adult and sometimes consist of angry outbursts or behavioral disturbances, and the reality that most children are still firmly entrenched in a family on whom they are dependent. When counseling the child, the above should be considered. It would be commoner (and often more appropriate) for the counselor to work with an adult member of the family, or with the family as a unit.

Specialists in the therapy of children utilise different forms of play therapy to help the younger child to express feelings. The older child may appreciate a more direct discussion of feelings, while the adolescent may benefit from a therapy group with peers with whom he can identify.

Black et al. (1987) found, in an intervention study in families where one of the parents had died, that treatment along the following lines was beneficial. The aims were to promote mourning in the children and the surviving parent and to improve family communication, particularly about the death. Intervention consisted of six sessions by trained bereavement counselors, who were also experienced psychiatric social workers, taking place in the family home within five months of bereavement. The events leading up to the death were reviewed with the family, looking at photographs and mementos, using techniques to encourage the expression of grief which included modelling of appropriate verbal behaviors and responses. This was often the first occasion in which the parent and children had sat down together and talked about their loss and their feelings about it. Sometimes it was necessary to see a parent alone for one or two sessions to deal with their needs separately.

The study by Kaffman et al. (1987) of children who had lost their fathers demonstrated a high level of pathological disturbance in the early months of bereavement, both in kibbutz and city children. They suggested that intervention focussing largely on the expression of grief, as is the nub of many approaches to adult grief counseling, is rather limited and should not be applied as a standard prescription in all cases. They suggested a balanced program, including preventative intervention, with recognition of the wide range of bereavement reactions in children, including the expression of grief or anger, hysterical identification with the deceased father, denial of death, and other more adaptive reactions. An adequate explanation of death to the child, the freedom to express emotions, the presence of a person with empathic understanding (often most appropriately the mother), the offer of support or consultation for the mother were all regarded as important during the first few weeks to months. During the first and second years of bereavement a stable and secure emotional environment, with the possibility of a substitute father figure, and a minimisation of environmental changes and stresses were regarded as important.

In addition to helping the bereaved child by meeting the needs of the parent, assisting family communication, and, if necessary, giving the child the opportunity to express himself, it is possible to enlist the help of schoolteachers and peers, who, given some understanding, can make the life of the child much more tolerable.

GRIEF COUNSELING IN THE DISABLED

Bereavement in groups such as the mentally handicapped, the chronic psychiatrically ill, and the chronic physically disabled person may have differing implications, result in different manifestations of grieving, and require different forms of intervention.

Mcloughlin (1986) has drawn attention to the grieving process in the mentally handicapped. The concept of death in this group is not related to age but to cognitive levels. The highest level of cognitive functioning in this group is at the concrete operational level, although some would be functioning at a more primitive level. It was suggested that those with a more sophisticated concept of death may be more vulnerable and less able to resolve their grief. When the person has been looked after at home by a relative for many years the degree of attachment may be very great, with catastrophic consequences on the loss of a caregiver. The denial of an opportunity to attend the funeral, communication problems such as deafness or poor speech, a very restricted social circle, removal from the failiar environment and other accompanying losses all compound the difficulties of grieving, with the consequence that many suffer from complicated grief reactions which may result in admission to a psychiatric unit (Day, 1985). Preparing the mentally handicapped for bereavement through educational and targeted groups, the way in which they are informed about a death, attending the funeral, minimising environmental changes and building up alternative avenues of support prior to a bereavement may all decrease the possibility of avoidable distress or complicated grief.

The chronic psychiatrically ill who are increasingly being cared for in the community as a result of social policies share some of the problems of the mentally handicapped in that they may become very dependent on their carers, have fewer coping resources, more communication problems, and fewer supportive social relationships. In addition, they may have already experienced rejection by part of the community. For a person who has only been coping in a marginal way in the community, the loss of a key relationship may precipitate hospital admission. The manifestations of grieving, with withdrawal, sleep disturbance, loss of appetite, and loss of interest may sometimes be misinterpreted as a relapse of a psychotic condition and inappropriately treated by increasing doses of medication, when grief counseling would be more beneficial.

The physically disabled who are less mobile and have relied extensively on a caring person for their needs may also be catastrophically affected by the loss of a carer. Opportunities to discuss the loss and feelings of grief are required, in addition to the provision of support for physical needs. The physically handicapped who are able to retain some independence and responsibility for their lives are more likely to grieve successfully.

Grief is no respecter of persons, however well endowed physically or mentally they may be, but those who have resources, are mobile, and have problem-solving skills are able to cope better with some aspects of loss, and remain protected while grieving and reestablishing their equilibrium.

GRIEF COUNSELING IN THE ELDERLY

The older bereaved person is more likely to be a widow then a widower, to have a less severe bereavement reaction with increasing age (Maddison et al., 1967), to experience more problems of grieving if the spouse suffers a lingering death (Vachon, 1976), and is less likely to demonstrate clearly marked stages of grief (Brink, 1985). While the experience of grief may be less intense in some elderly people, a considerable number still experience psychological and physical morbidity and are likely to require some help in working through feelings of grief, if blocked or severe. Bereavement in the elderly may be compounded by other losses, of physical functioning, sensation, social status, or material ones, which colour the presentation.

Essa (1986) discussed a technique of psychotherapy with elderly bereaved patients using Raphael's model of crisis intervention, addressing the affective, defensive, cognitive, reality, and object relations aspects, and suggested that primary care practitioners could readily be taught these techniques.

In addition to technique it is important to match a therapist who is perceived as congruent to the patient. An elderly patient complained to me that her bereavement counselor only wished to talk about one thing, namely grief, which the patient considered she had been dwelling on for long enough. She thought the counselor, who was younger than her granddaughter, would not have much understanding of grief and should have more cheerful things to put her mind to at her age.

The basic principles of bereavement counseling are applicable in the elderly as in any other adult group provided the counselor is aware that the ageing individual is more likely to suffer from a range of physical problems, may be isolated socially and may have suffered a number of other losses as outlined above.

Hysterical reactions occur more frequently in the very young and the elderly, which may be associated with a brain which has less functional reserve. Regressed behavior in the elderly bereaved in which the individual becomes petulant and demanding may also occur. The individual requires support but some limit-setting regarding the prolonged or extreme expression of emotions. It may emerge that the elderly widow (or widower) who manifests regressed behavior of this sort has had a chronic ambivalent relationship with their partner, and has often been very dependent. However, regressed behavior, if it persists, may require specialised investigation, for psychiatric disorder or a dementia.

If responsibilities for routine activities of living are taken over by a protective family for more than a short time, the individual, who may be physiologically aroused with undirected energy, may become frustrated, bored, and demoralised. There is an optimal amount of social support which is required in order to allow some time and energy for grieving, but without taking over the functioning of that person as a member of society.

GRIEF COUNSELING AFTER STILLBIRTH

As discussed previously, stillbirth, which is often unexpected, untimely, and very distressing for the parents who have built up expectations about a child, may result in complicated grief reactions. Condon (1986) discussed the therapy of established pathological grief, utilising a multi-disciplinary stance, which incorporated some aspects of developmental psychology and some of behavioral psychology. A careful history of the individual's obstetric history and her attitudes towards it, followed by a joint interview with the spouse consisting of visualisation of the baby and its whereabouts utilising cognitive strategies, the ventilation of feelings, interpreting transference where appropriate, particularly when termination of therapy was an issue and the utilisation of support groups, provided they did not exacerbate rage or grief on a chronic basis, were considered to be useful.

This area has become more widely recognised as a legitimate focus of therapy.

SPECIALISED DEVELOPMENTS IN GRIEF COUNSELING

Volkan (1980) described the development of "re-grief" therapy, in which a person who is arrested in a state of pathological mourning is assisted in working though grief by firstly taking a detailed history, in order to establish why the patient will not permit the deceased to die, using a psychodynamic framework, secondly focusing on the patient's "linking objects" (which are tokens of the dead person), encouraging the patient to bring these to the therapeutic session, to look at and to touch them, in order to stimulate memories of the deceased, and thirdly helping the patient to review the circumstances of the death and emotional reactions at the time. An abreaction of repressed emotion may then take place. Any transference feelings towards the therapist are quickly interpreted. The capacity of the individual to tolerate emotions is considered prior to the treatment. Reactions to earlier losses are reviewed. The therapist may accompany the patient on a visit to the grave.

"Re-grief" therapy appears to combine strands from psychodynamic psychotherapy, behavioral techniques (including desensitisation in vitro and flooding), and general supportive measures, with a focus on adapting to the loss of an important relationship.

Lieberman (1978) has described "forced mourning" whilst Mawson et al. (1981) made a controlled study of "guided mourning," in which twelve patients with morbid grief were randomly allocated to either guided mourning treatments, in which they were encouraged to repeatedly face cues concerning their bereavement, or to control treatment, in which they were asked to avoid such cues. After six sessions the guided mourning patients improved significantly more than the controls, this improvement being maintained at ten to twenty-eight week follow up. The active treatment consisted of exposure of the patient to avoided or painful memories, ideas or situations, both in imagination and in real life, related to the loss of the deceased. The patient was encouraged to describe repeatedly the areas which were most painful involving sadness or guilt, and to visit avoided places such as the hospital where the deceased died or the cemetery. When phobic avoidance mainly concerned the loss, the patient was encouraged to say "goodbye" to the deceased aloud in the sessions and in writing during "homework." During the first four sessions, patients were instructed to write one page daily on their relationship with the deceased, to think about the deceased as often as possible, and to look at a photo of the deceased daily. This treatment would certainly appear to confront the patient with the inescapable reality of the death and give an opportunity to ventilate some of the associated emotions in the presence of a therapist. It was suggested that guided mourning might possibly be indicated where grief had been avoided, repressed, or delayed.

Gauthier (1979) drew attention to the role of social reinforcement, the possible consequences of a conspiracy of silence with the resultant "incubation" of distress and an abnormal grief reaction. He described a graduated self-exposure program for the management of grief in a fifty year-old man with arteriosclerotic heart disease which had necessitated coronary bypass surgery, who had been experiencing a prolonged grief reaction following the death of his seventeen year old son who was killed in a motorcycle accident. His behavior consisted of avoidance activities such as never entering his son's room and avoiding thinking about his son. A hierarchy of these avoiding thinking activities was constructed and a graduated program of exposure to these activities was constructed combined with practicing self coping types of statement. The program was repeated on a twice daily basis with good results. Withdrawal of treatment resulted in a return of the previous avoidance activities, but further treatment produced gains which were maintained at the one year follow up. It was suggested that in some situations, flooding (prolonged exposure to high intensity stimuli) might be more effective than brief exposure to low intensity stimuli. However, flooding would not necessarily be advisable in a patient with severe coronary disease as an initial marked increase in sympathetic arousal could exacerbate the coronary disorder.

Melges et al. (1980) discussed grief resolution therapy which involved guided imagery, in which the patient views sequences of loss as though they were taking place in the present. The therapist helps the patient to revise the scene so that there are fewer inhibitions to full grieving. Dialogues with the deceased are encouraged. These techniques are similar to the Gestalt Therapy techniques, discussed by Smith (1985), in which the client is encouraged to carry on a dialogue with the deceased in an "empty chair" in order to express appreciation, resentment, and regret towards the deceased and complete the work of mourning.

The use of imagery has been discussed by Cerney (1985). Requesting the bereaved person to recall a dream, with eyes closed, about the deceased, may help to increase the awareness of subconscious material, and then work through the loss with the ability to finally let go of the deceased.

It is possible to use a combination of the above techniques and in practice this often occurs. Hodgkinson (1982) described the cathartic treatment of abnormal grief utilising a combination of "forced mourning" techniques, systematic desensitisation, stimulating negative emotions repeatedly in a hierarchical fashion until they are extinguished, response prevention, in which certain rituals to contact the deceased are prevented by the therapist, and Gestalt techniques, in which conflicts are identified and externalised by establishing a dialogue between the bereaved and the deceased.

Many of the therapies discussed so far for aiding people who are experiencing abnormalities of grieving appear to combine techniques which promote an active recall of the deceased, which is often anxiety provoking or painful initially but subsequently less so. In addition there is usually an encouragement of some abreaction of emotion and in some therapies consideration of conflicts in the relationship with the deceased, a working through of these conflicts and finally a letting go of the deceased. These maneuvres provoke responses which parallel the course of normal grieving and perhaps this is the ultimate aim. Angry feelings may be displaced onto the therapist. The patient may need support to accept that some of these feelings stem from resentment towards the deceased, which may need to be balanced against the idealisation of the deceased which often occurs.

Patients who seek dynamic psychotherapy are frequently coming to terms with situations of loss or early bereavement, and it could be argued that this type of treatment might be useful for those who are experiencing difficulty with a current bereavement. Horowitz et al. (1984) specifically utilised time limited dynamic psychotherapy in a study of fifty-two self-referred patients. The therapy was given over twelve sessions on a weekly basis, utilising interpretations of transference, interpretations about defensive maneuvres and a focus on the implications of the loss of the relationship to self-conceptualisation and the subsequent role relationships. The goal was to relieve distress by facilitating a normal rather than a pathological grief process and to differentiate between fantasy beliefs and the realistic appraisals of the actual implications of death. Confrontation, abreaction and catharsis all occurred in therapy where appropriate. This therapy promoted a substantial improvement in symptoms and to a lesser extent in social and work functioning. Other findings in this study indicated that exploratory actions were more helpful in highly motivated and better organised patients and less suitable for those who were less motivated or organised in self-concept, whilst more supportive actions were therapeutic for patients at lower dispositonal levels and less therapeutic for those at higher levels.

As in many other areas of counseling and psychotherapy, treatment must be adapted to meet the needs and personality of the patient in order to achieve an optimal result.

Individuals who do not respond to grief counseling, behavioral, Gestalt or short-term psychotherapy techniques as described above, may require more prolonged or far reaching psychotherapy. A deeply embedded pathological relationship with the deceased may interfere with the establishment of a relationship with a psychotherapist, as that would be a betrayal of the dead. In such a situation, it is possible that there have been earlier major deficits in relationships. Treatment, if it continues, may need to address issues of early deficits and their impact on object relations.

PSYCHOPHARMACOLOGIC AGENTS IN BEREAVEMENT

Suffering on its own is not a prerequisite for recovery from a bereavement. When suffering becomes excessive there is a tendency for all of us to try to suppress that suffering, whether through mental mechanisms such as those of denial or through diversion or through the use of drugs. If suffering is extreme, the individual may seek a way out through suicide.

There is a tendency for the bereaved, without any particular encouragement from the medical profession, to increase their intake of minor tranquillisers, hypnotics, alcohol, or other drugs, if they have previously been dependent on these substances. The use of psychotropic agents as a routine measure in uncomplicated bereavement is not recommended. It has been suggested that suppressing a bereavement reaction pharmacologically could lead to a delay in working through grief. A more well established drawback in the prolonged use of minor tranquillisers or hypnotics is the problem of dependence.

The insomnia which accompanies grieving in some individuals may be troublesome and exhausting and treatment with a modern hypnotic, such as a benzodiazepine derivative should be considered. The use of alcohol to promote sleep should be discouraged as the likelihood of middle and terminal insomnia is very high, and there are major potential problems with tolerance and dependence.

The characteristic symptoms of grief may resemble those of a depressive disorder, with depressed mood, tearfulness, anorexia, insomnia, and loss of interest in daily activities. Some patients are overaroused in the sympathetic nervous system, and may be hypervigilant, searching and experiencing subjective tension. However the course of a normal grief reaction usually shows a marked variation in the intensity and fluctuation of symptoms with the most dramatic symptoms subsiding within a few days to weeks. In addition, there is often intense preoccupation with the deceased, a need to talk about this, with a gradual response to social support and a tendency for the process to be self limiting. The routine use of antidepressants or anxiolytics in this situation is contraindicated in my opinion. The use of antidepressants would, in addition to the possibility of interfering with a normal grief reaction, tend to take too long to relieve the immediate symptoms of grief, as the antidepressant onset of action takes approximately two weeks. An additional drawback in the use of antidepressants is the side effect spectrum which may include tiredness, problems in concentration, dry mouth or constipation.

However, an animal model which supports the use of antidepressants in bereavement, separation and loss is suggested by the work of Mckinney et al. (1986). They showed that "depressive behavior" in primates which were separated from their mothers or siblings was alleviated by imipramine.

Persistent or severe depressive states in bereavement merit treatment with antidepressants. Jacobs et al. (1987) described a pilot study in which seven out of ten bereaved spouses who had a major depressive disorder showed moderate to marked improvement of depressive symptoms during a four week open trial of desipramine, a tricyclic antidepressant which was given in a nighttime dose of up to 150 mgs. Symptoms which responded most rapidly to this treatment were disturbances of sleep and appetite. It was suggested that pharmacologic treatments were important to evaluate as they are efficient, inexpensive, and within the armamentarium of the primary care physician.

Muskin et al. (1986) drew attention to the lack of empirical research to substantiate the efficacy of either psychotherapy or pharmacotherapy in normal and abnormal grief. They described a double blind placebo trial, in progress, of imipramine in bereaved widows who met the criteria for Major Affective Disorder.

Clinical experience confirms that patients who develop, postbereavement, classical depressive symptoms which persist, are troublesome and unresponsive to counseling, benefit from treatment with standard antidepressant regimes. The important questions are often not to do with a dichotomised approach utilising either psychotherapy or pharmacotherapy but involve judging when grief is becoming so severe or abnormal in spite of counseling or social support that further measures are required to help restabilise the neuroendocrine system. Following these biological approaches, counseling or psychotherapy may be reinstituted. The patient is then in a more receptive state of mind and is not swamped with anxiety or with an excess of negative thoughts, and is able to resume a working through of grief. The individual who has a previously established history of mood disorder should be carefully monitored during a bereavement in order to ascertain the possibility of a relapse.

With the advent of newer, pure serotonin re-uptake blocker antidepressants, it would be of interest to ascertain whether these are a more effective class of drug in the treatment of bereavement-related depressions.

This class of drugs shows some promise as a useful adjunct to analgesic regimes for the treatment of neuropathic pain, which I am currently studying. The affective pain of grief may also respond to this class of drug. It would be useful to construct a study comparing the efficacy of the serotonin re-uptake blocker antidepressants with that of the norepinephrine re-uptake blockers in bereavement-related depressions. It is possible, however, that the side effects of the former group, which include insomnia and anorexia which are often problems in grieving anyway, would be unacceptable to the patient.

CLINICAL VERSUS RESEARCH ISSUES

The key questions which have not been fully answered by researchers in the field include those of who will benefit most from bereavement counseling and what form that bereavement counseling should take. The question of when an individual whose grief has taken an abnormal course should receive more specialised treatment, involving psychotherapy, behavior therapy or pharmacotherapy, depends largely on clinical judgement, the attitudes of health professionals, and the resources available.

It would be inhumane to suggest that an individual in distress should be denied some comfort and in many situations following bereavement this is given spontaneously, intuitively and with good results. However, specific techniques administered by professionals to those bereaved who seek help or to those who are seen to be at risk may not always be a cost effective way of decreasing symptoms and in some instances could possibly prolong the course of grief.

Osterweis (1984) and Stroebe et al. (1987) reviewed intervention research on mutual support or psychotherapy for the bereaved. Studies have often relied on limited numbers of case studies, have not clearly indicated the treatment being given, have not included a nonintervention comparison group or have consisted of a self-selected sample. However, progress has been made and some of the more carefully conducted studies have given an indication of the therapeutic potential of different interventions.

Raphael (1977) found that preventive interventions were effective in the early bereavement period in those widows deemed to be at risk from perceived lack of social support, a previous highly ambivalent relationship with the deceased, and major concurrent life events. Treatment, consisting of four two hour sessions by a psychiatrist in the widow's home, resulted in an improvement rate of 77 percent whereas the untreated control group had an improvement rate of 41 percent at thirteen month post bereavement follow up. The key predictor of outcome appeared to be the perceived supportiveness of the social network.

Trained volunteers were used in the controlled study by Parkes (1979) at St. Christopher's Hospice which resulted in a better health outcome for the intervention group.

Vachon et al. (1980) utilised trained widow volunteers, who had resolved their own bereavement reactions, to offer emotional support and practical help to a group of 68 widows. The differences in adaptation between these women and a control group who were followed up for two years suggested that those receiving intervention followed the same general course of adaptation as control subjects, but that the rate of achieving landmark stages in intrapersonal adaptation and socialisation was accelerated in the intervention group.

Marmar et al. (1988) in a controlled trial of widows who sought treatment for unresolved grief reactions demonstrated that either brief dynamic psychotherapy with experienced clinicians or mutual-help group treatment led by nonclinicians resulted in a reduction in stress-specific and general symptoms as well as in improvement in social and work functioning. An apparent superiority of brief psychotherapy for one of the eleven outcome variables could have been accounted for by the greater attrition rate of subjects in the mutual-help group. It was suggested that each type of treatment addressed different needs of the patient, the group treatment placing greater emphasis on support, modelling and exchange of practical information, whereas brief psychotherapy emphasised the identification and resolution of recurrent maladaptive relationship patterns and idosyncratic obstacles to the mourning process.

Stroebe et al. (1987) maintain that the thrust of research supports their hypothesis that intervention reduces risk in those whose informal social network does not provide support, confirming their "deficit model." Social support may be the vehicle for a number of other therapeutic factors which reverberate with intrapsychic phenomena, in addition to enabling the provision of simple advice on daily living activities and providing some degree of companionship.

What seems irrefutable is that bereaved individuals experience distress and an increase in psychological symptoms for which they sometimes seek or may require help. Physical health may also be at risk during the time of intense grieving. Health professionals are going to be involved for different reasons and at different times with the bereaved. Those who become involved in administering bereavement counseling should be aware of the limitations and advantages of therapy, the natural course of grief, and the utility of trained volunteers. The personality attributes and training of volunteers requires consideration so that optimal, cost effective help can be given to the bereaved. Those who develop complicated grief reactions which do not respond to the help of trained volunteers need to be identified and referred to counselors or therapists who are able to assist using a range of techniques.

CHAPTER 16

LIVING WITH DYING

And therefore never send to know
for whom the bell tolls
It tolls for thee. . . .

John Donne

The way in which we grieve is influenced by our own attitude to death and especially our attitude to or fear of our own death. The dying of another person arouses anxieties about our own mortality. If we can view the death of a close relative as comfortable and dignified and can view them as achieving some peace or even personal growth, then our own fear of death is likewise diminished, and our grief over their demise is likely to be less traumatic.

If the fear of death is prominent and we fear either a tortuous afterlife or a terrible vacuum, then:

The weariest and most loathed worldly life
That age, ache, penury and imprisonment
Can lay on nature, is a paradise
To what we fear of death.

Measure for Measure III,i,127
William Shakespeare

However, Epicurus, in Roman times, reassured a society which was overanxious about a shadowy afterlife and a myriad of ghosts and superstitions, that there was no afterlife, that death was the end and comfort could be taken from the notion that after death there was nothing and no process of torment nor shadowy existence in Hades. From this stance he urged individuals to live life to the full and to be joyful whilst they were alive, as after death there was nothing. His advice has been misinterpreted to condone excesses and oversatiation—"Eat, drink and be merry, for tomorrow we die"—but that was not his intention.

148

A Confucian perspective is contained in the saying of Mencius (Meng Tsu) in 300 B.C.:

> Thus we see how life thrives with sorrow and calamities and perishes with ease and joy.

If life is a "vale of tears" and suffering is paramount, then death brings a welcome relief. It is not uncommon for consolations to be given to the bereaved such as "he was suffering so much, it was a welcome relief for him to slip away." Whilst this does not mitigate the initial pain of grief it provides one rationale with which to come to an acceptance of the death.

Sophocles, in a pessimistic mode declared that it was best of all never to have been born, and second best, if one has already made an appearance in the world, to go back again as quickly as possible.

Grief could be viewed as a phase in a relationship. The relationship is no longer with a living person, but is with one whose physical existence has ceased, but is still present in the mind of the bereaved. This highlights the need for an examination of the relationship of the bereaved with the deceased prior to death. Malinak et al. (1979) noted the importance of the last visit to the parent by adults who experience parental bereavement. This encounter sometimes acted as a "screen memory" for many aspects and issues of the parent-child relationship. The grieving may not be just over the loss of the deceased, but be a reactivation of grief over previous losses. Malan (1979) pointed out that the tears of some bereaved individuals may not really be in touch with the true process of mourning but may emanate from earlier unresolved infantile conflicts around the depressive position.

The attitudes of the dying person to his own death effect the approach of relatives and carers who respond accordingly. A desire to escape too rapidly from life may be experienced as a rejection by relatives. Denial of dying may create a dilemma for relatives who wish to review important personal issues with the dying person. At a material level, if denial of death is prominent, practical arrangements may not be made, a current will may not be prepared, with the creation of divisiveness and conflict amongst relatives subsequently.

Lifton et al. (1979) studied six Japanese men who were dying and examined their attitudes from historical, cultural, and psychological aspects. The sense of biological and historical connectedness and sense of immortality which these men were striving for did not appear to be simply a denial of death. It was thought that the desire for immortality could be achieved through a biological mode (having progeny), a religious mode (transcending death through spiritual power which did not necessarily incorporate an after life), creativity (living on through one's works), a Shinto belief in being part of eternal nature, and through experiential transcendence (achieving ecstasy, or "losing oneself"). These attitudes, although differing in content are not unlike many beliefs in Western cultures. The Shinto belief, which was echoed in the poetry of William Wordsworth has been taken up by the environmentalist lobby with great fervour, while experiential transcendence has become of great interest to Western devotees of meditation and those who attempt to achieve "peak experiences."

Attempts to circumvent death through physical means, modern technology or a belief in an afterlife or resurrection have all featured in Western civilisation.

The attitude of the dying to the funeral and other arrangements has repercussions on the bereaved. A desire to help humanity by donating bodily organs may be an attempt to cheat death, but may create conflict in relatives who then become unsure of the finality of the death. A desire for a "happy funeral" is sometimes expressed and may reflect the personality of the individual:

> Lodovicus Cortesius, a rich lawyer of Padua commanded by his last will, that no funeral should be kept for him, no man should lament; but as at a wedding, musick and minstrels to be provided; and, instead of mourners, he took order that twelve virgins clad in green should carry him to the church.
>
> *The Anatomy of Melancholie,*
> Robert Burton

Amongst the severely ill who are dying, psychiatric disorders are common. Massie et al (1987) noted in a study of two hundred and fifteen cancer patients that 47 percent received a DSMIII diagnosis, 32 percent had an adjustment disorder, 6 percent a major affective disorder, 4 percent an organic mental disorder, 3 percent a personality disorder and 2 percent an anxiety disorder. The importance of treating these conditions as well as relieving pain and physical suffering cannot be stressed too highly in order for the dying person to think and communicate in a state of clear consciousness with some degree of physical comfort. The input of specialists in palliative care and a high standard of medical, psychiatric, and supportive services in hospice care assists this process. If the dying person is in a hospital or hospice setting it is of importance for the family to avail themselves of the opportunity to spend time with him to promote final leave-taking and also to reduce possible guilt reactions. Physicians and nurses responsible should ensure that they remain in contact with the dying in order to provide comfort and security.

Throughout life we are preparing ourselves for losses. Anticipation of death may not be a pessimistic activity but a process which is personally reassuring:

> I will conclude with Epictetus; "If thou lovest a pot, remember 'tis but a pot thou lovest; and thou wilt not be troubled when it is broken; if thou lovest a son or wife, remember they are mortall; and thou wilt not be so impatient. . . . to resist and prepare ourselves not to faint, is best: 'tis a folly to fear that which cannot be avoided, or to be discouraged at all.

> *The Anatomy of Melancholie*
> Robert Burton

Carl Jung saw the acceptance of death in the latter half of the lifecycle as a life enhancing activity. He considered that from the middle of life onward, vitality of existence only came to those who were ready to "die with life" (Feifel, 1959). Kohut (1966) lists facing death as being one of the transformations of narcissism which represents a major step towards maturity and the integration of the self.

Returning to the fundamental aspects of grief, it appears to be a biological phenomenon which is deeply rooted in human experience as a response to loss, particularly to the loss of a bereavement. Descriptive studies of grief have corrected some misconceptions regarding the time scale and normal range of symptoms. Physiological, immunological, and endocrinological studies reveal interesting preliminary findings. An understanding of the mechanisms and expression of emotion in general is relevant to an understanding of grief.

The diverse psychological theories of grief provide some rationale for the processes which occur. It has not been clearly established whether the expression of emotion alone brings diminution in distress in the bereaved. However, many subjective reports attest to the benefits of communicating distress and reviewing the relationship with the deceased.

Social theories highlight the existence of man as a social animal and emphasise the reduction of distress of the bereaved given social support and highlight the possibility of increased risks of morbidity following spousal bereavement. In addition to social and cultural factors and dynamics, the previous personality, experiences and quality of the relationship interact to modify the course of grief.

The few controlled intervention studies with the bereaved have not convincingly established the efficacy of any particular approach although a number of empirically based approaches which offer social support and help to modulate the abnormal grief reaction and promote personal and social reintegration show promise.

The preparation of individuals through education about death, dying and grief which is neither dramatised, vulgarised, nor exploitative could commence in childhood. Opportunities for families to encounter death in the home have been reduced with modern medical and societal trends and on occasion this has transformed death into an artificial or dysjunctive situation occurring in an alien environment.

A description and understanding of the diverse phenomena of grief, which has been attempted in this book, requires the input of different sciences, some of which are still in their infancy, combined with some personal experience of loss and grieving. Any comprehensive overview of grief leads into the existential questions about the foundations of our being and the nature of suffering. Middleton et al. (1987) quote Vaillant who stated "Grief hurts, but does not make us ill. We forget that it is the inconstant people who stay in our lives who drive us mad, not the constant ones who die. We forget that it is failure to internalize those whom we have loved, and not their loss, that impedes adult development."

Ultimately, there may be a turning away from grief, although the memories still remain.

> We will grieve not, rather find
> Strength in what remains behind;
> In the primal sympathy
> Which having been must ever be;
> In the soothing thoughts that spring
> Out of human suffering;
> In the faith that looks through death,
> In years that bring the philosophic mind.

Ode on Intimations of Immortality
From Recollections of Early Childhood.
William Wordsworth

BIBLIOGRAPHY

Aberbach, D. Grief and mysticism. *International Review of Psychoanalysis*, 14, 509–526, 1987.

Alarcon, R.D. Personality disorder as a pathogenic factor in bereavement. *Journal of Nervous and Mental Disorder*, 172, 45–47, 1984.

Albert, R. Cognitive development and parental loss among the gifted, the exceptionally gifted and the creative. *Psychological Reports*, 29, 19–26, 1971.

Ambelas, A. Psychologically stressful events in the precipitation of manic episodes. *British Journal of Psychiatry*, 135, 15–21, 1979.

Anthony, S. *The Discovery of Death in Childhood and After.* New York: Basic Books, 1972.

Auslander, G. Bereavement research in Israel—a critical review of the literature. *Israel Journal of Psychiatry and Related Sciences*, 24, 33–51, 1987.

Averill, J. Autonomic response patterns during sadness and mirth. *Psychophysiology*, 5, 339–414, 1969.

Bak, R. Being in love and object loss. *International Journal of Psychoanalysis*, 54, 1–8, 1973.

Bartrop, R., Lazarus, L., Luckhurst, E., Kiloh, L. and Penny, R. Depressed lymphocyte function after bereavement. *Lancet*, 16th April, 834–836, 1977.

Bean, W. *Rare Diseases and Lesions. Their Contributions to Clinical Medicine.* Springfield: Charles C Thomas, 1967.

Beck, A., Rush, A., Shaw, B. and Emery, G. *Cognitive Therapy of Depression.* New York: Guildford, 1981.

Bentovim, A. Bereaved children. *British Medical Journal*, 292, 1482, 1986.

Black, D. Pathological laughter. A review of literature. *Journal of Nervous and Mental Disease*, 170, 67–71, 1982.

Bleuler, R. *Textbook of Psychiatry.* (Trans. by A.A. Brill), New York: Macmillan, 1924.

Bowlby, J. The Making and Breaking of Affectional Bonds. 1. Aetiology and psychopathology in the light of attachment theory. *British Journal of Psychiatry*, 130, 201–210, 1977.

Bowlby, J. *The Making and Breaking of Affectional Bonds.* London: Tavistock, 1979.

Bowlby, J. *Attachment and Loss: Vol. 3.* New York: Basic Books, 1980.

Breier A., Kelsoe, J., Kirwin, P., Beller, S., Wolkwitz, O. and Pickar, D. Early parental loss and development of adult psychopathology. *Archives of General Psychiatry*, 45, 987–993, 1988.

Brink, T.L. The grieving patient in later life. *Psychotherapy Patient*, 2, 117–127, 1985.

153

Brown, G. and Harris, T. *Social Origins of Depression: A Study of Psychiatric Disorder in Women.* London: Tavistock, 1978.

Brown, G., Harris, T. and Copeland, J. Depression and Loss, *British Journal of Psychiatry,* 130, 1–18, 1977.

Burns, E., House, J. and Ankenbauer, M. Sibling grief in reaction to sudden infant death syndrome. *Paediatrics,* 78, 485–487, 1986.

Burton, R. *The Anatomy of Melancholie.* New York: Tudor, 1960.

Butler, R. The life review: an interpretation of reminiscence in the aged. *Psychiatry,* 26, 65–76, 1963.

Cerney, M. Imagery and grief work. *Psychotherapy Patient,* 2, 35–43, 1985.

Childe, V.G. Directional changes in funerary practices during 5000 years. *Man,* 45, 16–18, 1945.

Christie, M. and McGrath, M. Taking up the challenge of grief: film as therapeutic metaphor and action ritual. *A.N.Z. Journal of Family Therapy,* 8, 193–199, 1987.

Clayton, P.J. Mortality and morbidity in the first year of widowhood. *Arch. Gen. Psychiatry,* 30, 747–750, 1974.

Clayton, P. Weight loss and sleep disturbance in bereavement. In *Bereavement Counseling. A Multidisciplinary Handbook.* Ed: Schoenberg B., Westport, Conn: Greenwood Press, 1980, pp. 72–77.

Clayton, P., Halikas, J. and Maurice, W. The bereavement of the widowed. *Diseases of the Nervous System,* 32, 592–604, 1971.

Condon, J. Management of established pathological grief reaction after stillbirth. *American Journal of Psychiatry,* 143, 987–997, 1986.

Corney, R. and Horton, F. Pathological grief following spontaneous abortion. *American Journal of Psychiatry,* 131, 825–827, 1974.

Cousins, N. *The Anatomy of an Illness.* New York: Norton, 1979.

Darwin, C. *The Expression of Emotions in Man and Animals.* London: Murray, 1872.

Day, K. Psychiatric disorder in middle aged and the elderly mentally handicapped. *British Journal of Psychiatry,* 147, 665–668, 1985.

DeSpelder, L. and Strickland, A. *The Last Dance: Encountering Death and Dying.* Palo Alto, Calif: Mayfield, 1987.

Deutsch, H. The absence of grief. *Psychoanalytic Quarterly,* 6, 12–22, 1937.

D.S.M.IIIR. Diagnostic and Statistical Manual of Mental Disorders. (Third Edition Revised). Washington: American Psychiatric Association, 1987.

Dubin, R. and Sarnoff, J. Sudden unexpected death: intervention with the Survivors. *Annals of Emergency Medicine,* 15, 54/99–102/57, 1986.

Duchowny, M. Pathological disorders of laughter. In *Handbook of Humor Research Vol II.* Eds: McGhee, P. and Goldstein, J., New York:Springer-Verlag, 1983, pp. 89–108.

Dyregrov, A. and Matthiesen, S. Similarities and differences in mothers' and fathers' grief following the death of an infant. *Scandinavian Journal of Psychology,* 28, 1–15, 1987a.

Dyregrov, A. and Matthiesen, S. Anxiety and vulnerability in parents following the death of an infant. *Scandinavian Journal of Psychology,* 28, 16–25, 1987b.

Dyregrov, A. and Matthiesen, S. Stillbirth, neonatal death and sudden infant death

(SIDS): perinatal reactions. *Scandinavian Journal of Psychology*, 28, 104–114, 1987c.

Eisenbruch. M. Cross cultural aspects of bereavement. II: Ethnic and cultural variations on the development of bereavement practices. *Culture, Medicine and Psychiatry*, 8, 315–347, 1984.

Eisenstadt, J. Parental loss and genius. *American Psychologist*, 33, 211–223, 1978.

Elias, N. *The Loneliness of the Dying.* Oxford: Basil Blackwell, 1985.

Engel, G. Is grief a disease? *Psychosomatic Medicine*, 23, 18–22, 1961.

Erikson, E. *Childhood and Society.* New York: Norton, 1963.

Essa, M. Grief as a crisis: psychotherapeutic interventions with elderly bereaved. *American Journal of Psychotherapy*, XL, 243–251, 1986.

Faravelli, C., Webb, T., Ambonetti, A., Fonnesu, F. and Sessarego, A. Prevalence of traumatic early life events in 31 agoraphobic patients with panic attacks. *American Journal of Psychiatry*, 142, 1493–1494, 1985.

Feifel, H. (Ed.) *The Meaning of Death.* New York: McGraw-Hill, 1959.

Fernandez-Marina, R. The Puerto Rico Syndrome: its dynamics and cultural determinants. *Psychiatry*, 24, 79–82, 1961.

Finkelstein, M. The long term effects of early parent death: a review *Journal of Clinical Psychology*, 44, 3–9, 1988.

Fisch, R.Z. Alexithymia, masked depression and loss in a holocaust survivor. *British Journal of Psychiatry*, 154, 708–710, 1989.

Fisher, S. and Fisher, R. Personality and psychopathology in the comic. In *Handbook of Humor Research, Vol II.* Eds: McGhee, P. and Goldstein, J. New York: Springer-Verlag, 1983, pp. 41–59.

Fleming, J. and Altschul, S. Activation of mourning and growth by psychoanalysis. *International Journal of Psychoanalysis*, 44, 419–431, 1963.

Frankel, S. and Smith, D. Conjugal bereavement amongst the Huli people of Papua New Guinea. *British Journal of Psychiatry*, 141, 302–305, 1982.

Freud, A. Discussion of Dr. John Bowlby's paper. *Psychoanalytic Study of the Child*, 15, 53–62, 1960.

Freud, S. (1917) Mourning and melancholia. In *Standard Edition Vol XIV,* London: Hogarth Press, 1957.

Furman, E. *A Child's Parent Dies.* New Haven: Yale University Press, 1974.

Furman, E. Children's patterns in mourning the death of a loved one. In *Childhood and Death.* Eds: Wass, H. and Corr, C. Washington: Hemisphere, 1984, pp. 185–203.

Furman, R. Death and the young child. *Psychoanalytic Study of the Child*, 19, 321–333, 1964.

Garb, R., Bleich, A. and Lerer, B. Bereavement in combat. *Psychiatric Clinics of North America*, 10, 421–436, 1987.

Gardner, A. and Pritchard, M. Mourning, mummification and living with the dead. *British Journal of Psychiatry*, 130, 23–28, 1977.

Gauthier, J. and Pye, C. Graduated self-exposure in the management of grief. *Behaviour Analysis and Modification*, 3, 202–208, 1979.

Glick, I., Weiss, R. and Parkes, C. *The First Year of Bereavement.* New York: Wiley Interscience, 1974.

Goody, J. *Death, Property and the Ancestors: A Study of the Mortuary Customs of the Lo Dagaa of West Africa.* Stanford: Stanford University Press, 1962.

Gorer, G. The pornography of death. In *Modern Writing.* Eds: Phillips, W. and Rahv, P., New York: McGraw Hill, 1959.

Gorer, G. *Death, Grief and Mourning in Contemporary Britain.* London: Cresset Press 1965.

Greenblatt, M. The grieving spouse. *American Journal of Psychiatry*, 135, 43–46, 1978.

Gregory, I. Anterospective data following childhood loss of a parent. a) Delinquency and high school dropout; b) Pathology, performance and potential among college students. *Archives of General Psychiatry*, 13, 99–109, 110–120, 1965.

Griffin, G.M. and Tobin, D. *In the Midst of Life... The Australian Response to Death.* Melbourne: Melbourne University Press, 1982.

Hafner, R. and Roder, M. Agoraphobia and parental bereavement. *Australian and New Zealand Journal of Psychiatry*, 21, 340–344, 1987.

Haig, R. *The Anatomy of Humor: Biopsychosocial and Therapeutic Perspectives.* Springfield: Charles C Thomas, 1988.

Helsing, K. and Szklo, M. Mortality after bereavement. *American Journal of Epidemiology*, 114, 41–52, 1981.

Hickie, I. and Silove, D. A family panics. *Australian and New Zealand Journal of Psychiatry*, 23, 418–421, 1989.

Hirsch, J., Hofer, M. and Holland, J. Toward a biology of grieving. In *Bereavement Reactions, Consequences and Care.* Eds: Osterweis, M., Solomon, F. and Green, M. Washington, D.C.: National Academy Press, 1984, pp. 145–174.

Hofer, M. Relationships as regulators: a psychobiological perspective on bereavement. *Psychosomatic Medicine*, 46, 183–197, 1984.

Horowitz, M., Marmar, C., Weiss, D., DeWitt, K. and Rosenbaum, R. Brief psychotherapy of bereavement reactions. The relationship of process to outcome. *Archives of General Psychiatry*, 41, 438–448, 1984.

Horowitz, M.J., Wilner, N., Marmar, C. and Krupnick, J. Pathological grief and the activation of latent self images. *American Journal of Psychiatry*, 137, 1157–1162, 1980.

Irwin, M., Daniels, M. and Weiner, H. Immune and neuroendocrine changes during bereavement. *Psychiatric Clinics of North America*, 10, 449–465, 1987.

Jackson, C. Death shall have no dominion: the passing of the world of the dead in America. In *Death and Dying: Views from Many Cultures.* Ed: Kalish, R., New York: Baywood, 1980, pp. 47–55.

Jackson, E. Grief and religion. In *The Meaning of Death.* Ed: Feifel, H., New York: McGraw Hill, 1959, pp. 218–233.

Jacobs, S., Mason, J., Kosten, T. et al. Bereavement and catecholamires. *Journal of Psychosomatic Research*, 30, 489–496, 1986.

Jacobs, S., Nelson, J. and Zisook, S. Treating depressions of bereavement with antidepressants. A pilot study. *Psychiatric Clinics of North America*, 10, 3, 501–510, 1987.

Jacobs, S. and Ostfeld, A. An epidemiological review of the mortality of bereavement. *Psychosomatic Medicine*, 39, 344–357, 1977.

Jacobsen, R.H. Unresolved grief of 25 years duration exacerbated by multiple subsequent losses. *Journal of Nervous and Mental Disease,* 174, 624–627, 1986.

Jacome, D.E., Maclain, L.W., and Fitzgerald, R. Postural reflex gelastic seizures. *Archives of Neurology,* 37, 249–251, 1980.

Jaffe, L. and Jaffe, A. Terminal candor and the coda syndrome. *American Journal of Nursing,* 1976, 1938–1940.

Jandolo B., Gessini, L., Occhipinti, E. and Pompili, A. Laughing and running fits as manifestation of early traumatic epilepsy. *European Neurology,* 15, 177–182, 1977.

Janson, M. The prescription to grieve. *Hospice Journal,* 1, 103–109, 1985.

Jaques, E. Death and the mid-life crisis. *International Journal of Psychoanalysis,* 46, 502–514, 1965.

Jones, D. Cancer mortality and widow(er)hood in the Office of Population Censuses and Surveys: Longitudinal Study. In *Psychosocial Oncology.* Eds: Watson, M., Greer, S. and Thomas, C. Oxford: Pergamon, 1987, 33–42.

Kaffman, M., Elizur, E. and Gluckson, L. Bereavement reactions in children: therapeutic implications. *Israel Journal of Psychiatry and Related Sciences,* 24, 65–76, 1987.

Keddie, K.M. Pathological mourning after the death of a domestic pet. *British Journal of Psychiatry,* 131, 21–25, 1977.

Kitson, G. and Zyzanski, S. Grief in widowhood and divorce. *Psychiatric Clinics of North America,* 10, 369–386, 1987.

Klein, M. Mourning and its relation to manic depressive states. In *Contributions to Psychoanalysis* 1921–1949, London: Hogarth Press, 1948.

Kohut, H. Forms and transformations of narcissm. *Journal of the American Psychoanalytical Association,* 14, 243–272, 1966.

Koocher G.P. Childhood, death and cognitive development. *Developmental Psychology,* 9, 369–375, 1973.

Kraepelin, E. *Dementia praecox and paraphrenia.* Edinburgh: Livingstone, 1919.

Kramer, H.C. Laughing spells in patients after lobotomy. *Journal of Nervous and Mental Disease,* 119, 517–522.

Krell, R. and Rabkin, L. The effects of sibling death on the surviving child: a family perspective. *Family Process,* 18, 471–477, 1979.

Krupp, G. Identification as a defence against anxiety in coping with loss. *International Journal of Psychoanalysis,* 46, 303–314, 1965.

Laudenslager, M. The psychobiology of loss: lessons from humans and nonhuman primates. *Journal of Social Issues,* 44, 10–36, 1988.

Lazare, A. Unresolved grief. In *Outpatient Psychiatry: Diagnosis and Treatment.* Ed: Lazare, A. Baltimore: Williams and Wilkins, 1979, pp. 498–512.

Leavesley, J.H. *Medical By-Laws: Famous Diseases and Diseases of the Famous.* Sydney: Collins, 1984.

Leopold, N.A. Gaze induced laughter. *Journal of Neurology.* Neurosurgery and Psychiatry, 40, 815–817, 1977.

Lewis, E. and Page, A. Failure to mourn a stillbirth: an overlooked catastrophe. *British Journal of Medical Psychology,* 51, 237–241, 1978.

Lifton, R., Kato, S. and Reich, M. *Six Lives Six Deaths, Portraits from Modern Japan*. New Haven and London: Yale University Press, 1979.

Lindemann E. Symptomatology and management of acute grief. *American Journal of Psychiatry*, 101, 141–148, 1944.

Lishman, W.A. *Organic Psychiatry*. Oxford: Blackwell, 1978.

Lopata, H. Time in anticipated future and events in memory. *American Behavioral Scientist*, 29, 695–709, 1986.

Lopez, T. and Kliman, G. Mourning in the analysis of a 4 year old. *Psychoanalytic Study of the Child*, 34, 235–271, 1979.

Lukas, C. and Seiden, H. *Silent Grief: Living in the Wake of Suicide*. New York: Charles Scribner's Sons, 1988.

Maddison, D. and Viola, A. The health of widows in the year following bereavement. *Journal of Psychosomatic Research*, 12, 297–306, 1968.

Maddison, D.C. and Walker, W.L. Factors affecting the outcome of conjugal bereavement. *British Journal of Psychiatry*, 113, 1057–1067, 1967.

Mahler, M. On the first three subphases of the separation individuation process. *International Journal of Psychoanalysis*, 53, 333–338, 1972.

Malan, D. *Individual Psychotherapy and the Science of Psychodynamics*. London: Butterworths, 1979.

Malinak, D., Hoyt, M. and Patterson, V., Adults' reactions to the death of a parent: a preliminary study. *American Journal of Psychiatry*, 136 1152–1156, 1979.

Mandelbaum, D. Social uses of funeral rites. In *The Meaning of Death*. Ed: Feifel, H., New York: McGraw Hill, 1959, 189–217.

Marmar, C., Horowitz, M., Weiss, D., Wilner, N. and Kaltreider, N. A controlled trial of brief psychotherapy and mutual-help group treatment of conjugal bereavement. *American Journal of Psychiatry*, 145, 203–209, 1988.

Marris, P. *Loss and Change*. New York: Pantheon, 1974.

Martin, J. Psychological consequences of AIDS-related bereavement among gay men. *Journal of Consulting and Clinical Psychology*, 56, 856–862, 1988.

Massie, M. and Holland, J. The cancer patient with pain: psychiatric complications and their management. *Medical Clinics of North America*, 71, 243–258, 1987.

Mathers, J. The gestation period of identity change. *British Journal of Psychiatry*, 125, 472–474, 1974.

Maurer, A. Maturation of concepts of death. *British Journal of Medical Psychology*, 39, 35–41, 1966.

Mawson, D., Marks, I., Ramm, L. and Stern, R. Guided mourning for morbid grief: a controlled study. *British Journal of Psychiatry*, 138, 185–193, 1981.

McGhee, P.E. and Goldstein, J.H. (Eds) *Handbook of Humor Research Vol I and II*. New York: Springer-Verlag, 1983.

Mckinney, W. Primate separation studies: relevance to bereavement. *Psychiatric Annals*, 16, 281–287, 1986.

Mcloughlin I.J. Bereavement in the mentally handicapped. *British Journal of Hospital Medicine*, 256–260, 1986.

Meares, R. On saying goodbye before death. *Journal of the American Medical Association*, 246(11), 1227–1229, 1981.

Melges, F. and DeMaso, D. Grief resolution therapy: reliving, revising and revisiting. *American Journal of Psychotherapy*, XXXIV, 51–61, 1980.

Middleton, W. and Raphael, B. Bereavement. State of the art and state of the science. *Psychiatric Clinics of North America*, 10, 329–343, 1987.

Mor, V., McHorney, M.A. and Sherwood, S. Secondary morbidity among the recent bereaved. *American Journal of Psychiatry*, 143, 158–163, 1986.

Murray, J. and Callan, V. Predicting adjustment to perinatal death. *British Journal of Medical Psychology*, 61, 237–244, 1988.

Muskin, P. and Rifkin, A. Tricyclic antidepressants in the treatment of depression in conjugal bereavement: a controlled study. In *Pain, Anxiety and Grief*. Eds: Goldberg, I., Kutscher, A., New York: Columbia University Press, 1986, 200–209.

Nagy, M. The child's theories concerning death. *Journal of Genetic Psychology*, 73, 3–27, 1948.

Nicol, M., Tompkins, J., Campbell, N. and Syme, G. Maternal grieving response after perinatal death. *Medical Journal of Australia*, 144, 287–289, 1986.

Nicholas, A. and Lewin, T. Grief reactions of parental couples; congenital handicap and cot death. *Medical Journal of Australia*, 144, 292–298, 1986.

Nightingale, A. Unresolved grief presenting with features of a negative therapeutic reaction. *British Journal of Psychiatry*, 155, 862–864, 1989.

Osterweis, M., Solomon, F., Green, M. *Bereavement: Reactions, Consequences and Care*. A Report of the Institute of Medicine, National Academy of Sciences, Washington, D.C.: National Academy Press, 1984.

Parker, G. and Manicavasagar, V. Childhood bereavement circumstances associated with adult depression. *British Journal of Medical Psychology*, 59, 387–391, 1986.

Parkes, C. Components of the reaction to loss of a limb, spouse or home. *Journal of Psychosomatic Research*, 16, 343–349, 1972.

Parkes, C. Evaluation of a bereavement service. In *The Dying Human*. Eds: De Vries, A. and Carmi, I., Ramat Gan, Israel: Turtledove, 1979, 389–402.

Parkes, C. *Bereavement*. London: Penguin, 1980.

Parkes, C. Bereavement. *British Journal of Psychiatry*, 146, 11–17, 1985.

Parkes, C. Bereavement as a psychosocial transition: processes of adaptation to change. *Journal of Social Issues*, 44, 53–65, 1988.

Parkes, C. and Brown, R. Health after bereavement. *Psychosomatic Medicine*, 34, 449–461, 1972.

Parkes, C. and Weiss, R. *Recovery from Bereavement*. New York: Basic Books, 1983.

Paul, N. *The use of empathy in the resolution of grief*. Perspectives in Biology and Medicine, 10, 409–418, 1967.

Paul, N. The paradoxical nature of the grief experience. *Contemporary Family Therapy*, 8, 5–19, 1986.

Peppers, L. and Knapp, R. Maternal reactions to involuntary fetal/infant death. *Psychiatry*, 43, 155–159, 1980.

Piaget, J. *The Child and Reality—Problems of Genetic Psychology*. New York: Grossman, 1973.

Phuntso, C. Customs and rituals of the Tibetans. In *Tibet*, Ed: Tomasevic M. et al, New York: McGraw Hill, 1981, pp. 88–94.

Pigman, G. *Grief in Literature:* Grief and English Renaissance Elegy. Cambridge: Cambridge University Press, 1985.

Podell, C. Adolescent mourning: the sudden death of a peer. *Clinical Social Work,* 17, 64–78, 1989.

Poeck, K. Pathophysiology of emotional disorders associated with brain damage. In *Handbook of Clinical Neurology.* Eds: Vinken, P., Bruyn, G., Vol 3, Amsterdam: North Holland, 1969, pp. 343–367.

Raphael, B. Preventive intervention with the recently bereaved. *Archives of General Psychiatry,* 34, 1450–1454, 1977.

Raphael, B. The young child and the death of a parent. In *The Place of Attachment in Human Behavior.* Eds: Parkes, C. and Stevenson-Hinde, J., London: Tavistock, 1982.

Raphael, B. *The Anatomy of Bereavement,* New York: Basic Books, 1983.

Raskin, M., Peeke, H., Dickman, W. and Pinsker, H. Panic and generalised anxiety disorders. *Archives of General Psychiatry,* 39, 687–689, 1982.

Rees, W. The hallucinations of widowhood. *British Medical Journal,* 4, 37–41, 1971.

Reid, J. A time to live, a time to grieve; patterns and processes of mourning among the Yolngu of Australia. *Culture, Medicine and Psychiatry,* 3, 319–346, 1979.

Rosenblatt, P.C. *Bitter, Bitter Tears: Nineteenth Century Diarists and Twentieth Century Grief.* Minneapolis: University of Minnesota Press, 1983.

Rosenman, S.J. and Tayler, H. Mania following bereavement: a case report. *British Journal of Psychiatry,* 148, 468–470, 1986.

Roy, A. Early parental separation and adult depression. *Archives of General Psychiatry,* 42, 987–991, 1985.

Roy, A. Role of past loss in depression. *Archives of General Psychiatry,* 38, 301–302, 1981.

Roy, A. Vulnerability factors and depression in women. *British Journal of Psychiatry,* 133, 106–110, 1978.

Rush, B. *Medical Inquiries and Observations upon the Diseases of the Mind.* Philadelphia: Grigg and Elliott, 1835.

Rutter, M. Bereaved children. In *Children of Sick Parents.* Maudsley Monograph XVI, Oxford: Oxford University Press, 1966, 66–75.

Rynearson, E. Psychological adjustment to unnatural dying. In *Biopsychosocial Aspects of Bereavement.* Ed: Zisook, S. Washington, D.C.: American Psychiatric Press, 1987, pp. 75–93.

Savin, D. The expression of mourning in an 8 year old girl. *Clinical Social Work Journal,* 15, 121–135, 1987.

Schleifer, S., Keller, S., Camerino, M., Thornton, J. and Stein, M. Suppression of lymphocyte stimulation following bereavement. *Journal of the American Medical Association,* 250, 374–377, 1983.

Scully, E.J. Men and grieving. *Psychotherapy Patient,* 2, 95–100, 1985.

Sekaer, C. Towards a definition of childhood mourning. *American Journal of Psychotherapy,* XLI, 201–219, 1987.

Sher, P.K. and Brown, J.B. Gelastic epilepsy. *Am. J. Dis. Child.,* 130, 1126–1131, 1976.

Sifneos, P. The prevalence of "alexithymic" characteristics in psychosomatic patients. *Psychother. Psychosom.* 22, 255–262, 1973.

Simpson, M.A. *Dying, Death and Grief.* Pittsburgh: University of Pittsburgh, 1987.

Smith, E. A gestalt therapist's perspective on grief. *Psychotherapy Patient*, 2, 65–78, 1985.

Smith, J. Identificatory styles in depression and grief. *International Journal of Psychoanalysis*, 52, 259–266, 1971.

Snowdon, J., Solomons, R. and Druce, H. Feigned bereavement: twelve cases. *British Journal of Psychiatry*, 133, 15–19, 1978.

Spitz, R. Hospitalism: An inquiry into the genesis of psychiatric conditions in early childhood. *Psychoanalytic Study of the Child*, 2, 53–74, 1945.

Spitz, R. Anaclitic depression. *Psychoanalytic Study of the Child*, 2, 313–342, 1946.

Stengel, E. *Suicide and Attempted Suicide.* Harmondsworth: Penguin, 1969.

Stroebe, M. and Stroebe, W. Who suffers more? Sex differences in health risks of the widowed. *Psychological Bulletin*, 93, 279–301, 1983.

Stroebe, W. and Stroebe, M. *Bereavement and health. The psychological and physical consequences of partner loss.* Cambridge: Cambridge University Press, 1987.

Sugar, M. Normal adolescent mourning. *American Journal of Psychotherapy*, 22, 258–269, 1968.

Tennant, C. Parental loss in childhood. *Archives General Psychiatry*, 45, 1045–1050, 1988.

Tennant, C., Hurry, J. and Bebbington, P. The relation of childhood separation experiences to adult depressive and anxiety states. *British Journal of Psychiatry*, 141, 475–482, 1982.

Tennant, C., Smith, A., Bebbington, P. and Hurry, J. Parental loss in childhood. *Archives of General Psychiatry*, 38, 309–314, 1981.

Theut, S., Pedersen, F., Zaslow, M., Cain, R., Rabinovich, B. and Morihisa, J. Perinatal loss and parental bereavement. *American Journal of Psychiatry*, 146, 635–639, 1989.

Thielman, S. and Melges, F. Julia Rush's Diary: coping with loss in the early nineteenth century. *American Journal of Psychiatry*, 143, 1144–1148, 1986.

Thorson, J. and Powell, F. Elements of death anxiety and meanings of death. *Journal of Clinical Psychology*, 44, 691–701, 1988.

Torgersen, S. Childhood and family characteristics in panic and generalised anxiety disorders. *American Journal of Psychiatry*, 143, 630–632, 1986.

Tudehope, D., Iredell, J., Rodgers, D. and Gunn, A. Neonatal death: grieving families. *Medical Journal of Australia*, 144, 290–292, 1986.

Tweed, J., Schoenbach, V., George, L. and Blazer, D. The effects of childhood parental death and divorce on six-month history of anxiety disorders. *British Journal of Psychiatry*, 154, 823–828, 1989.

Vachon, M. Grief and bereavement following the death of a spouse. *Canadian Psychiatric Association Journal*, 21, 35–44, 1976.

Vaillant, G. *Adaptation to Life.* Boston: Little Brown, 1977.

Van Eerdewegh, M., Bieri, M., Parrilla, R. and Clayton, P. The bereaved child. *British Journal of Psychiatry*, 140, 23–29, 1982.

Van Eerdewegh, M., Clayton, P., Van Eerdewegh, P. The bereaved child: variables influencing early psychopathology. *British Journal of Psychiatry*, 147, 188–194, 1985.

Volkan, V. The linking objects of pathological mourners. *Archives of General Psychiatry*, 27, 215–221, 1972.

Volkan, V. "Re-Grief" Therapy. In *Bereavement Counseling: A Multidisciplinary Handbook*. Ed: Schoenberg, B., Westport, Conn: Greenwood Press, 1980, 334–350.

Wahl C. The fear of death. In *The Meaning of Death*. Ed: Feifel, H., New York: McGraw Hill, 1959, pp. 214–223.

Warnes, H. Alexithymia and the grieving process. *Psychiatric Journal of the University of Ottawa*, 10, 41–44, 1985.

Wass, H. Concepts of death. A developmental perspective. In *Childhood and Death*. Eds: Wass, H. and Corr, C. Washington: Hemisphere, 1984, 3–24.

Weinberg, N. The health care social worker's role in facilitating grief work: an empirical study. *Social Work in Health Care*, 10(3), 107–117, 1985.

Weiss, R. Loss and recovery. *Journal of Social Issues*, 44, 37–52, 1988.

Williams, M., Schutt, W. and Savage, D. Epileptic laughter with precocious puberty. *Arch. Dis. Child*, 53, 249–251, 1980.

Wilson, S.A.K. Some problems in neurology. II: Pathological laughing and crying. *Journal of Neurology and Psychopathology*, 4, 299–333, 1924.

Windholz, M., Marmar, C. and Horowitz, M. A review of the research on conjugal bereavement: impact on health and efficacy of intervention. *Comprehensive Psychiatry*, 26, 433–447, 1985.

Wolfenstein, M. Loss, rage and repetition. *Psychoanalytic Study of the Child*, 24, 432–460, 1969.

Wolff, C., Hofer, M. and Mason, J. Relationship between psychological defenses and mean urinary 170HCS excretion rates. II: Methodological and theoretical consideration. *Psychosomatic Medicine*, 26, 592–609, 1964.

Worden, J.W. *Grief Counseling and Grief Therapy*. New York: Springer, 1982.

Wright, A., Cousins, J. and Upward, J. *Matters of Death and Life: A Study of Bereavement Support in N.H.S. Hospitals in England*. London: Kings Fund, 1988.

Yalom, I. *Existential Psychotherapy*. New York: Basic Books, 1980.

Yamamoto, J., Okonogi, K., Iwasaki, T. and Yoshimura, S. Mourning in Japan. *American Journal of Psychiatry*, 125, 1660–1665, 1969.

Yates, T. and Bannard, J. The "haunted" Child: grief, hallucinations and family dynamics. *Journal of the American Academy of Child and Adolescent Psychiatry*, 27, 573–581, 1988.

Zisook, S. Unresolved grief. In *Biopsychosocial Aspects of Bereavement*. Ed: Zisook, S., Washington, D.C.: American Psychiatric Press, 1987, 21–34.

Zisook, S. and Shuchter, S. The first four years of widowhood. *Psychiatric Annals*, 16, 288–294, 1986.

Ziv, A. *Personality and Sense of Humor*. New York: Springer, 1984.

ADDENDUM TO BIBLIOGRAPHY

Hodgkinson, P.E. Abnormal grief—the problem of therapy. *British Journal of Medical Psychology,* 55, 29–34, 1982.

Lampl de Groot, J. On the process of mourning. *Psychoanalytic Study of the Child,* 38, 9–13, 1983.

Lieberman, S. Nineteen cases of morbid grief. *British Journal of Psychiatry,* 132, 159–163, 1978.

Silverman, S. Parental loss and scientists. *Science Studies,* 4, 259–264, 1974.

Woodward, W. Scientific genius and the loss of a parent. *Science Studies,* 4, 265–277, 1974.

AUTHOR INDEX

165

Wass, H., 70, 76, 162
Webb, T., 155
Weinberg, N., 129, 162
Weiner, H., 156
Weiss, D., 158
Weiss, R., 19, 110, 155, 159, 162
Williams, M., 35, 162
Wilner, N., 156, 158
Wilson, S.A.K., 30, 31, 34, 35, 162
Windholz, M., 11, 162
Wolfenstein, M., 75, 77, 79, 93, 162
Wolff, C., 27, 162
Wolkowitz, O., 153
Worden, J.W., 109, 133, 162
Wright, A., 116, 118, 162
Woodward, W., 100, 163

Wordsworth, W., 152

Y

Yalom, I., 13, 74, 86, 162
Yamamoto, J., 60, 162
Yates, T., 84, 162
Yoshimura, S., 162

Z

Zaslow, M., 161
Zisook, S., 9, 108, 156, 162
Ziv, A., 40, 162
Zyzanski, S., 157

SUBJECT INDEX

ABOUT THE AUTHOR

Doctor Robin Haig is a consultant psychiatrist currently practicing in Sydney, Australia and lecturing at Sydney University. He trained in medicine and psychiatry at King's College Hospital, London, and later at the Tavistock Clinic. Doctor Haig was also the Director of Clinical Psychiatric Services at the Royal Hobart Hospital, Tasmania and Director of Psychiatry in the Macarthur Area, Sydney.

His interests are in the areas of psychotherapy, change and loss, palliative care psychiatry and thanatology, grief counseling and the role of humor in human transactions. He was a founder member of the Tasmanian Psychoanalytically Oriented Group, the Psychotherapy Association of Australia and has served as a member on the Board of Continuing Education of the Royal Australian and New Zealand College of Psychiatrists.

His previous book, *The Anatomy of Humor*, complements this current volume.

DATE DUE